Introduction to Currency Risk

INTRODUCTION TO CURRENCY RISK

Brian Coyle

FINANCIAL WORLD Publishing

BPP FINANCIAL EDUCATION

Financial World Publishing
c/o The Chartered Institute of Bankers
Emmanuel House
4-9 Burgate Lane
Canterbury
Kent
CT1 2XJ
United Kingdom

Telephone: 01227 762600

Financial World Publishing publications are published by
The Chartered Institute of Bankers, a non-profit making registered educational charity.

Typeset by Kevin O'Connor
Printed by Leggo Spa, Italy

ISBN 0-85297-432-9

Contents

Financial Risk

Risk arises from uncertainty *now* about what might happen in the *future*. The perception of risk is often defensive, anticipating negative rather than positive outcomes. For example, when preparing for a foreign business trip you might envisage

- the airplane crashing (accident risk)
- falling ill before or during the trip (health risk)
- being held up in traffic and missing the plane (traffic risk)
- flight delay (delay risk)
- having money stolen (theft risk).

This simple example illustrates the defensive attitude we take to risk, and also the tendency we have to categorize *types* of risk.

Commercial Risk and Financial Risk

Risk is inevitable in business, and the success or failure of its risk management will affect a company's profits. Business risk falls broadly into two categories, commercial and financial risk.

Commercial risk relates to the business environment in which a company operates and is the risk of a downturn or setback in business conditions. For example

- sales of a new product could fall short of expectation
- market share could be lost to a rival product
- the supply of raw materials could be interrupted.

Financial risk is the possibility of changes in financial conditions in the future that will affect revenues or costs. Currency risk is one type of financial risk.

Categories of Financial Risk

The term *exposure* that can be defined as *exposure to risk*, describes the existence of a financial risk for a business. There are different types of financial risk including

- country risk, sub-categorized into economic, political and regulatory risk
- price risk
- credit risk and counterparty risk
- interest rate risk
- currency risk, or exchange rate risk.

Country Risk

Country risk arises from cross-border transactions, when a business in one of the countries might suffer higher costs or lower profits because of *future* changes in the economic, political or regulatory environment in the other country. Risk is much greater in some countries than in others; for example, a long-term transaction in Hong Kong might be a greater risk than a long-term transaction in Singapore because it reverted to Chinese control in 1997.

Another example of country risk would be giving credit to a customer in a developing country with a foreign currency shortage. A new government might impose further foreign exchange restrictions in response to deteriorating economic conditions. A combination of economic, political and regulatory changes would have adverse financial consequences for the company granting the credit. It might not be able to receive payment from its customer, even though the customer would be able and willing to pay the debt.

Economic, political and regulatory conditions are significant factors in country risk.

Economic Risk

Fluctuations in a country's economic environment, such as wage levels, inflation and the rate of growth or recession, will affect the costs and revenues of companies operating there.

Example

XYZ Inc exports goods from the US priced in dollars and competes in world markets with German producers, who price their goods in euros.

Analysis

There might be a risk that unit costs of production in the US will increase at a higher rate than in Germany, caused perhaps by higher wage settlements or declining productivity in XYZ's industrial sector. If the euro/dollar rate remains fairly stable, XYZ would be at risk of becoming less competitive against its German rivals because of the unfavorable economic conditions in the US compared with Germany. To remain competitive, XYZ Inc would have to

- keep its dollar prices static in spite of higher unit costs, therefore reducing profitability, or
- raise its dollar prices and become less competitive than German firms.

Political Risk

Political events can disrupt a company's business and thus have an effect on its profits. For example

- wars and similar disturbances. The invasion of Kuwait by Iraq in 1990, followed by the Gulf War in 1991, affected many companies adversely, particularly those trading with customers or suppliers in the war zone. The Gulf War also discouraged

international travel, and airlines suffered a sharp fall in business. On the other hand, in the dispute between NATO and Yugoslavia over Kosovo in 1999, some small airline companies benefited from a demand for their services by NATO forces to move people to and from countries near the war zone
- a political coup. For example, at the time of the break-up of the Soviet Union, there was a coup against President Gorbachev in August 1991, followed by a counter-coup several days later. These events caused a sharp fall in the value of the deutschemark, followed by an equally sharp recovery. This was because prospects for the German economy were thought at the time to be dependent on economic reforms and developments in central and eastern Europe. The deutschemark's value continued to fluctuate with the political uncertainty in Russia after the break-up of the Soviet Union
- a general moratorium on repayment of debt to foreign suppliers, declared by the government of a less developed country (LDC) or other country
- the nationalization of a company's assets by government
- elections, and the prospect of a change in government, might have an adverse effect on interest rates or exchange rates
- government-inspired measures to ban or restrict imports from particular countries. For example, trade disputes between the US and the European Union have given rise to import bans and the threat of further banning measures between the disputing governments.

Regulatory Risk

Regulatory bodies may make decisions that will have an impact on a company's profits. There is regulatory risk associated with

- listed companies on stock exchanges, new share issues, etc
- takeovers or mergers
- accounting and taxation
- other aspects of company law

- banks, the effects of which may be passed on to companies.

Economic, political and regulatory risk can exist at the same time, making business activity a high-risk operation. This has been evident, for example, in Russia since the collapse of the USSR. Foreign companies dealing with Russian customers, suppliers and joint venture partners have had to face high inflation, a weak market economy, an underdeveloped banking system, foreign exchange controls and political unrest.

Price Risk

Price risk is an exposure to a loss from the change in value of a commodity or financial instrument. Where the commodity or instrument is traded on an organized market, e.g. stocks and shares, price risk is also referred to as *market risk*.

For example, an investor in the shares of a public company can expect the share price to rise or fall, depending largely on

- changes in future prospects for profits and dividends
- changes in the yield available on alternative investments, e.g. a rise or fall in interest rates.

Occasionally there can be a large and unforeseen change in the level of stock market prices. In 1987 and 1989 for example, there were sudden and unforeseen falls in share prices, notably in the US and the UK. In contrast, in the late 1990s, the rise in shares on several stock markets, most notably the US, was bigger than fundamentals might seem to justify.

Credit Risk

Companies that give credit face the risk of non-payment or late payment, resulting in

- bad debt losses

- interest costs, or cost of carry, having to fund debtors for a longer time than intended
- administrative costs of chasing up late payers.

Counterparty Risk
A counterparty is the other party to a contract. There could be a risk that the counterparty will fail to honor his/her contract obligations. The risk of non-payment of money owed, i.e. credit risk, is a common form of counterparty risk.

Interest Rate Risk

When a company borrows or lends funds it is exposed to financial risks associated with the volatility of interest rates.

Interest rate risk is the risk from changes in market interest rates of either

- paying more in interest charges for borrowed funds than need have been paid, or
- receiving less interest income from deposits or loans in the case of banks than could have been earned.

Interest rate risk also arises from borrowing or investing in different currencies. Market rates of interest vary between currencies. You might borrow in one currency and then find in retrospect that it would have been cheaper to borrow in another. This *currency of denomination exposure* combines interest rate risk and currency risk.

Currency Risk (Exchange Rate Risk)

Currency risk, also referred to as exchange rate risk and foreign exchange risk, is the risk from adverse movements in exchange rates. When a company has assets or liabilities denominated in a foreign currency, or contracts to receive or pay in a foreign currency, it has an exposure to that currency.

An adverse movement in the exchange rate can affect a company by

- reducing its cash income
- increasing its cash expenditures
- reducing its reported profits
- reducing the reported value of its foreign assets
- increasing the value of its foreign currency liabilities
- damaging its competitive position in its domestic and foreign markets to the advantage of foreign rivals.

Cash flows are at risk from adverse exchange rate movements because

- companies that receive income in foreign currency often will wish to exchange it into domestic currency. For example, a French company that receives $50,000 for selling equipment to Saudi Arabia might wish to convert the dollars into euros
- companies with debts in a foreign currency will have to convert domestic currency into the foreign currency, i.e. buy currency, to pay what they owe

Currency risk to cash flows arises because of movements in the prices, or exchange rates, at which foreign currency is converted.

Profits also are at risk if they are earned by foreign subsidiaries. A UK company, for example, might earn annual profits of $600,000 from a US subsidiary. If the sterling/dollar exchange rate moves from £1 = $1.50 to £1 = $2.00, the value of the annual profits will slide from £400,000 to £300,000. In much the same way, the value of the assets of foreign subsidiaries, expressed in the parent company's domestic currency, is at risk from adverse exchange rate movements.

A company's competitiveness in both domestic and international markets can be under threat from currency risk.

Example
There are two producers of radios, one based in the EU and one in Singapore. The European company's production costs are €10 per unit and the Singapore company's S$20. The product sells for $15.

If current exchange rates are €1 = $1, €1 = S$2 and $1 = S$2, the two companies will be equally cost-competitive in world markets. Each company would incur the equivalent of $10 in costs and earn the equivalent of $5 profit per unit. The European company's profit would be €5 per unit and the Singapore company's profit would be S$10 per unit.

Analysis
Suppose, however, that the euro increased in value to €1 = $1.2 and €1 = S$2.4. The European company would now lose competitiveness. Its costs of €10 per unit would be equivalent to $12, and its unit profit of $3 would earn only €2.50 when converted to euros. The Singapore company's profits would be unaffected, giving it a considerable cost advantage over its European rival.

If the market had been the euro zone of the European Union, rather than the world, and goods had been priced in euros instead of dollars, much the same analysis could be made. A European producer always will be under a greater threat from foreign competition when the value of the euro increases against other currencies.

Currency risk is most clearly evident in the businesses of companies that buy or sell abroad. It also exists for any company that competes against foreign producers in its domestic market, or that uses foreign suppliers for materials, equipment and services.

In the sections that follow, the nature of currency risk and its consequences will be explored in greater depth.

Exposures

Specific financial risks are referred to as *exposures* that normally can be quantified.

- If a UK company is owed £1 million by a customer, it has a credit exposure of £1 million.
- If a UK company has borrowed £2 million at a floating rate of interest, it has an interest rate exposure of £2 million to a rise in interest rates.
- A non-US company that has sold goods abroad for $3 million but has not been paid, has both a credit exposure and a currency exposure for income of $3 million.

The Management of Risk

A company that faces financial risk might take measures to reduce or eliminate it. This is called *hedging* the exposures.

Companies have to accept some exposures to risk. Credit risk cannot be avoided unless a company refuses to grant credit to its customers. Similarly, an investor cannot avoid price risk unless he refuses to invest.

Management must decide how much exposure to risk is acceptable, and take measures to control or hedge the excessive risk. Occasionally, a company might seek to take on risk, in the hope of making speculative profits from favorable rate or price movements.

Two-Way Nature of Risk

Risk is exposure to change when the size, direction or timing of any future changes is uncertain. Change often can be favorable rather than adverse, and a company can profit from an exposure to financial risk whenever a change is favorable.

Suppose for example that a UK investor holds shares in a French company that have a market value of €1 million.

If the euro weakens in value against sterling, the sterling value of the investment will fall, and the investor will make a loss in sterling. On the other hand, if the euro strengthens against sterling the value of the shares in sterling will rise and the investor will make a profit from the currency movement.

Generally, the management of most non-financial companies are *risk averse*, i.e. they tend to avoid risk unless there is a reasonable expectation of higher profits. In other words, many companies often will prefer the certainty of a small profit rather than an exposure to financial risk that could mean a bigger profit but also the possibility of a loss.

Hedging Exposures

There are several methods and treasury instruments that can be used for hedging financial risks. A company should

- first identify the financial risks
- identify the various methods, including treasury instruments, for hedging these risks
- select the most suitable.

Not all exposures are hedged, even by large multinational companies. Cover should be sought and taken only when it seems worthwhile. However, a decision not to hedge should be a positive one. A company's management ought to know what its exposures are, and be able to recognize the alternatives for reducing them. It is fine not to hedge an exposure, but this should be a considered decision, not a passive hope that the exposure will resolve itself.

Exposures can be complex and difficult to identify, particularly in multinational companies. Increasingly, as financial markets and treasury instruments have developed, centralized corporate treasury departments have evolved to manage financial risk.

The treasury function involves

- managing cash flows, such as credit facilities and investment of surplus cash, and
- protecting assets and profits from financial risk.

Controlling Financial Risks

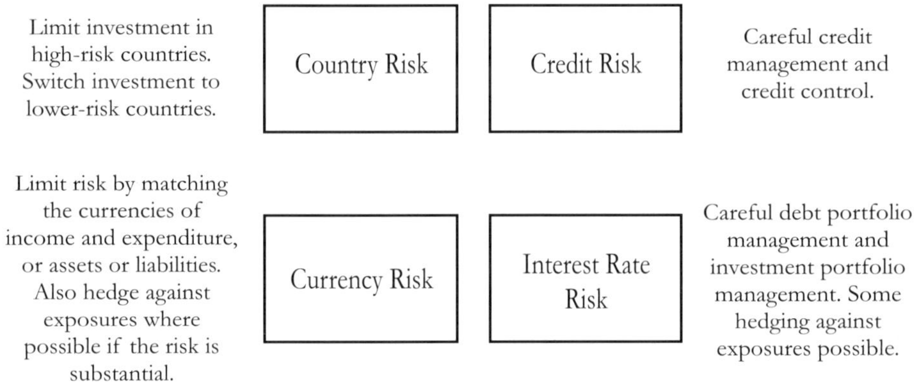

2

Currency Risk

Exchange rates are market rates for buying and selling quantities of one currency in exchange for another. The foreign exchange markets, or FX markets, exist to meet the demand and supply for currencies arising from cross-border trading, investment and other financial transactions.

Currency risk arises for organizations involved, directly or indirectly, in international trade and finance because

- exchange rates are volatile, in both the short and the long term
- future movements in exchange rates cannot be predicted accurately
- companies have exposures to foreign currencies, and will suffer losses, or loss of business, as result of adverse exchange rate movements.

How Exchange Rates are Determined

Exchange rates are continually changing, according to the strength of supply and demand for each currency in the FX markets. Supply and demand for currency is created by

- trade flows
- long-term flows of capital
- short-term speculative flows of capital.

In addition exchange rates can be controlled to some extent by official intervention from central banks that can buy or sell a currency in the FX markets to strengthen or weaken its value. Typically, a central bank will buy its domestic currency in the FX markets when the currency is falling in value, using the government's reserves of foreign currencies to pay for the purchases.

Exchange controls also can be imposed by governments restricting or prohibiting foreign exchange transactions involving their domestic currency. Such restrictions may help a government to control the currency's value by regulating the volume of supply or demand in the FX markets.

Both long-term and short-term factors influence the demand for buying and selling currency. The long-term trend in exchange rates is driven by economic fundamentals. The short-term trend is driven in the main by market sentiment, and other short-term supply and demand factors.

Fluctuations in Exchange Rates

Exchange rates can fluctuate widely over the long and the short term.

The graph below illustrates the long-term volatility in the sterling/dollar exchange rate between 1967 and 1997.

Until the arrival of the euro, the most heavily traded currencies in the foreign exchange markets were the dollar and the deutschemark. The exchange rate between these two currencies fluctuated by large amounts. For example, during the four-month period between April and August 1992, the dollar weakened by about 18% against the deutschemark, from about $1= DM1.65 to about $1 = DM1.40. It then strengthened over the next four months to stand at $1 = DM1.62 at the year end.

Although the euro was expected to bring more stability to exchange rates, in the three months after its introduction in January 1999, it fell in value against the dollar by about 10%.

The long-term trend in an exchange rate can affect the strategic position of a company in its markets. For example, for a UK company competing in world markets against US firms, any long-term trend towards a weaker

Sterling/Dollar Rate 1967-1997

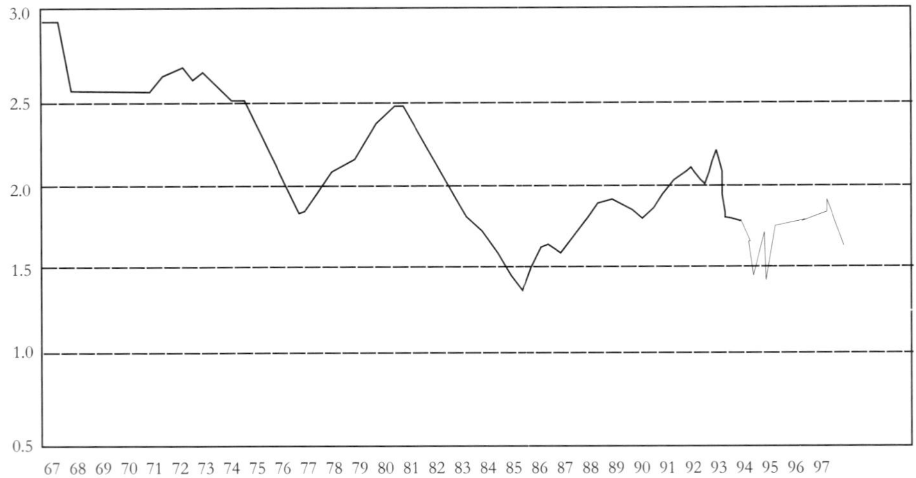

24-hour Sterling/Dollar Rate

dollar and a stronger pound would put the company at a cost disadvantage and, therefore, a price disadvantage also, enabling its US rivals to win market share at the company's expense.

Short-term Currency Risk

Exchange rates also change continuously throughout each working day because worldwide foreign exchange markets operate around the clock. Exchange rate movements can be considerable, even within minutes.

The graph reproduced opposite shows the trading range in the sterling/dollar exchange rate within a typical day. The timing of a transaction *within the day* can have a direct effect on profits, as shown by the following example.

Example
The treasurer of a UK company wants to buy $5 million. At 10 a.m. the sterling/dollar exchange rate is 1.5100, and $5 million would cost £3,311,258.28. At 3 p.m. the exchange rate is 1.5250, and $5 million would cost only £3,278,688.53. Therefore, favorable timing could save over £32,500 in one working day, whereas unfavorable timing could cost over £32,500.

Currency risk or exchange rate risk arises in buying, selling, investing and borrowing. Therefore, it is essential to recognize the nature of currency risks and how they arise in business.

Risks in Selling Abroad

A company selling goods or services abroad faces currency risk, regardless of whether its sales are priced in its domestic currency or in a foreign currency. For example, suppose that a UK company sells goods to foreign buyers.

Sales priced in sterling: if sterling strengthens, prices to foreign buyers in their domestic currency will rise. Demand will fall to an extent that will depend on the strength, or elasticity, of demand for the product. Falling sales will reduce total profits.

Sales priced in a foreign currency: if exports are priced in a currency that falls in value against sterling, the company's sterling earnings will fall. Profit margins also will fall. The company either must accept the lower profit margins or raise prices. Higher prices could result in lower sales demand and lower profits.

Risks in Buying from Abroad

A company buying goods from abroad might be invoiced in its domestic currency, but is more likely to be invoiced in a foreign currency. For example, suppose that a US company buys a range of goods from foreign suppliers.

Purchases invoiced in dollars: if the dollar weakens, foreign suppliers are likely to raise their dollar prices so that profits in their own currency can be maintained. Costs of purchases therefore will rise.

Purchases invoiced in a foreign currency: if the dollar weakens, it will cost the company more in dollars to buy the foreign currency to pay for the goods. Costs of purchases will rise.

Risks from Investing Abroad

The profits of a parent company's foreign subsidiary, as reported in the parent company's domestic currency, will fall if the subsidiary's domestic currency weakens in value against the parent company's domestic currency. As a result multinational companies with foreign subsidiaries have constant exposure to currency risk.

The value of a foreign investment will fall if the currency in which it is denominated weakens against the investor's domestic currency.

Institutional Investors

Institutional investors, such as insurance companies and pension funds, hold widely diversified portfolios of investments in different currencies. For example, they will hold shares and bonds of foreign companies. A risk for institutional investors is that the value of a company in which they invest could fall because of an adverse exchange rate movement. For example, a US investment institution might hold shares in a European company whose market value is €2 billion. If the euro/dollar exchange rate changes from €1 = $1.10 to €1 = $1.00, the European company's value in terms of dollars would fall by $200 million from $2.2 billion to $2 billion. The US investor would have made a loss.

Risks from Borrowing in a Foreign Currency

Exchange rate movements, as well as interest rates, affect the cost of borrowing in a foreign currency. The cost of a foreign currency loan will rise or fall if the borrower's domestic currency weakens or strengthens against the currency in which the loan is denominated.

Currency risk would be reduced if either

- the volatility in exchange rate movements were lessened and exchange rates were fairly stable, or
- future exchange rate movements could be predicted with reasonable accuracy.

Risk and Volatility

Currency risk depends on the regularity and size of exchange rate movements. An exposure to currency risk is greater when the exchange rate could change by a larger percentage amount, i.e. when exchange rate volatility is high. Changes that might occur in the future can be estimated from changes that have occurred in the past.

Example
A UK company borrows Swiss francs and dollars. It borrows SFr250,000 and $150,000 when the exchange rates for sterling against the Swiss franc and the dollar are SFr2.50 and $1.50 respectively. The loan principal is repayable after two years in both cases.

Suppose that during the past 12 months, the average exchange rate for the Swiss franc against sterling has been SFr2.49 and the rate has fluctuated between SFr2.47 and SFr2.52. The sterling/dollar exchange rate has averaged $1.48, and fluctuated between $1.42 and $1.56.

Analysis
The variation in the sterling/Swiss franc rate has been lower than the variation in the sterling/dollar rate over the past 12 months.

	Sterling/Swiss franc	**Sterling/dollar**
Range of variation	SFr0.05	$0.14
	(SFr2.52-SFr2.47)	($1.56-$1.42)
Average rate	SFr2.49	$1.48
Variation as a percentage of average rate	2.1%	9.5%

On the basis of the exchange rates in the past 12 months, the company's exposure to its dollar liability, the dollar loan, is greater than its exposure to the Swiss franc loan. The sterling cost of repaying both loans, at the current exchange rates of SFr2.50 and $1.50 to £1, would be £100,000. With both loans, there is a likelihood that the actual cost in sterling of repaying the loan principal in two years' time will be either higher or lower than £100,000.

Because the dollar exchange rate has been more volatile during the past 12 months, it is likely that the cost in sterling of repaying the dollar loan will differ from £100,000 by a larger amount than the cost in sterling of repaying the Swiss franc loan. In other words, the currency risk is greater with the dollar loan.

In this example, risk was measured by the ratio of variations in the exchange rate to the average exchange rate over a period of time. In practise, risk, price volatility, can be measured statistically as the standard deviation of exchange rate movements over a period of time.

Exchange Rate Stability

Currency risk is lower when exchange rates are fairly stable. If exchange rates could be fixed, currency risk would not exist at all. Stable exchange rates, by reducing the risks for participants, should provide a stimulus to international trade and finance.

Various attempts have been made to establish a system of stable exchange rates between major currencies.

The Gold Standard

From about 1880 until the outbreak of the First World War in 1914, exchange rates between major currencies were fixed by the Gold Standard. The main feature of the Gold Standard was the fixing of a currency's value in relation to gold. Two types of Gold Standard were applied

- a Gold Specie Standard, and
- a Gold Bullion Standard.

Under a Gold Specie Standard, gold coins are used as a medium of exchange and payment. The import and export of gold is unrestricted; gold bullion can be converted into coin on demand and gold coins can be melted down into bullion. Gold also is used to settle international payments.

Under a Gold Bullion Standard, gold coins are replaced wholly or in part by paper. Gold is held as a reserve asset by banks but paper money can be converted into gold on demand at the bank that issued the banknote. Only a small proportion of notes will be presented for exchange into gold, so banks can issue more paper money than they hold gold.

Because each currency has a fixed value in terms of gold, exchange rates are stable. International payments can be settled either in gold or a currency that has a fixed value against gold. Currency risk should be negligible. Under a Gold Standard, balance of payments surpluses or deficits result in the movement of gold between countries.

After the First World War, high rates of inflation in industrialized countries undermined the Gold Standard that finally collapsed in the mid-1930s. Many major currencies became either overvalued or undervalued against their gold parity, resulting in severe price distortions between countries. Corrective action, usually the devaluation of an overvalued currency, undermined exchange rate stability. From 1931 onwards, several countries introduced exchange controls.

The Bretton Woods Agreement (1944-1970)

Towards the end of the Second World War, an international conference at Bretton Woods in New Hampshire accepted a US proposal for a return to a form of Gold Standard. Under the so-called Bretton Woods system

- each member country set a parity value for its currency against the dollar and gold, and undertook to use central bank intervention to maintain the exchange rate within 1% of its parity
- the dollar's value against gold was fixed at $35 an ounce, and the US government undertook to buy or sell gold in exchange for dollars at this fixed rate.

As a result of the convertibility of the dollar into gold, a regime of stable exchange rates was established, and the dollar became the principal currency for the settlement of international transactions.

The Bretton Woods system was broadly successful for many years. However, during the late 1950s and the 1960s, the system was destabilized by a series of large devaluations or revaluations of several major currencies, including the French franc, deutschemark, guilder and sterling. The eventual collapse of the system of fixed exchange rates followed a loss of confidence in the dollar, leading to a decision by the US government to abandon the convertibility of the dollar into gold.

Under the subsequent Smithsonian Agreement (1971-1973) the exchange rates between major currencies were re-aligned, and an attempt was made at continuing with a system of fixed exchange rates. This proved unsupportable. Exchange rates could not be stabilized in the face of large international trade imbalances and movements of capital.

Industrialized countries moved to a system of floating exchange rates in 1973 because a fixed exchange rate system could not be sustained.

The Exchange Rate Mechanism (ERM)

The Exchange Rate Mechanism of the European Monetary System was developed to provide some stability in exchange rates between member currencies. Prior to September 1992, member currencies were the deutschemark, French franc, Dutch guilder, Belgian franc, sterling, lira, punt, Danish krone, peseta and the escudo. The pound and the lira were suspended from the ERM in September 1992.

Currencies in the ERM had fixed central rates against each other and against the ecu, a composite European currency, but a variation margin around the central rate was permitted before central government intervention was required.

Example
Suppose that the central rate for the deutschemark (DM) against the French franc (Fr) was as follows

DM/Fr	Fr/DM
Fr3.45 = DM1	Fr1 = DM0.289

Suppose also, as was the case, that a 2% margin of variation around the central rate was permitted.

Analysis

The permitted variations in the exchange rate before central government intervention was required would have been as follows

	DM/Fr	**Fr/DM**
Upper intervention point (+2%)	3.528 (approx)	0.296 (approx)
Central rate	3.450	0.289
Lower intervention point (-2%)	3.372 (approx)	0.283 (approx)

Because all member currencies within the ERM had to remain within the permitted variation margin against each other's currency, it followed that currencies could not rise by more than the maximum permitted variation margin against the weakest currency in the system. For example, if the maximum permitted variation for every member currency were 2%, no currency could rise in value by more than 2% above its central rate against the weakest currency in the system and therefore by a lesser amount against the other currencies.

Until 1992/93, the ERM was expected to establish a reasonable degree of exchange rate stability between the member currencies.

However, exchange rate stability cannot be maintained in the long term when the economy of one or more of the countries is weak. A government can raise interest rates to sustain the value of its currency, but only for a limited period without further damaging the economy.

In the case of sterling, its value in 1990-92 against other ERM currencies was unsustainable because of the weakness of the UK economy. The pressure for a re-alignment of exchange rates within the ERM, intensified by speculative trading on the foreign exchange markets, threatened the whole system with collapse during 1992 and 1993.

- In September 1992, speculation against sterling and the lira forced both currencies out of the ERM.

- Between September 1992 and May 1993, the peseta three times, the escudo twice, and the Irish punt once, were devalued against the other ERM currencies.
- In August 1993, further speculation against the French and Belgian francs and the Danish krone forced the EC authorities to permit wider fluctuations in the exchange rates between the remaining eight currencies in the system. Fluctuations of up to 15% on either side of the central rate were now permitted, compared to the 2% margins that applied previously to most of the currencies.

Subsequently the ERM recovered, and some exchange rate stability was restored. This revitalized system, referred to as ERM2, was a necessary forerunner of monetary union within the European Union and the introduction of the euro. In the months leading up to the introduction of the euro, exchange rates between the currencies of the participating countries were fixed, and no variations at all were permitted.

It is worth noting that

- although currency unions can try to create exchange rate stability for member currencies, exchange rates between member currencies and non-member currencies can remain volatile. The euro/dollar rate, for example, has been volatile since the euro's introduction in 1999.
- There is a risk that a currency inherently weak on economic fundamentals, e.g. sterling during the period 1990-1993, will be tied to a strong currency, the deutschemark, thus creating a proxy hard currency backed by a weak (UK) economy. This situation is difficult to sustain without damaging the weak economy still further.
- There could be a risk of an occasional devaluation or revaluation of a weak currency within the exchange rate system if its value against other member currencies cannot be contained within permitted limits. This was the experience of the ERM in 1992/93.

Economic and Monetary Union (EMU) and the Euro

In January 1999, 11 countries of the European Union (Austria, Belgium, Finland, France, Germany, Ireland, Italy, the Netherlands, Luxembourg, Portugal and Spain) entered into arrangements for Economic and Monetary Union, or EMU. There are various aspects to EMU, including a single central bank, the European Central Bank, and a single currency, in this case the euro.

Factors Influencing Exchange Rates (Supply and Demand for a Currency)

Long Term

- Interest rates. An increase in interest rates will attract more investment from abroad; investors will sell other currencies to buy investments in the currency offering a higher yield.
- Balance of trade on current account. Foreign trade in goods and services creates demand for currencies to pay for them.
- Inflation rate. A higher rate of inflation will make a country's currency less attractive because of the loss of real value that accompanies inflation.
- Economic conditions and related political conditions. Stronger economies attract more investors, leading to increased demand for its currency.
- Government intervention. To some extent, governments and central banks can intervene in FX markets to influence the exchange rate of their currency. In some cases, governments might co-operate to influence the value of a particular currency by buying or selling currency using their official reserves of foreign currency.

Short Term

- These variations, that are continuous, are influenced by short-term supply and demand conditions, but more particularly by market sentiment, a function of regular re-evaluation by market players of a combinaton of the long-run factors described above.

Can Future Exchange Rates Be Predicted?

Currency risk would be greatly reduced if future movements in exchange rates could be predicted. It might be argued that traders in the foreign exchange markets have access to enough information about currencies to predict how exchange rates will move, and build these predictions into the forward rates at which they buy and sell currencies.

In the FX markets, currencies are traded

- spot at the current exchange rate for immediate settlement, more exactly for settlement after two working days, and
- forward, for settlement at some time in the future.

Exchange rates for forward transactions differ from the current spot rate, and could be either higher or lower. For example, the spot rate for the dollar against sterling might be £1 = \$1.60, and the rate for a forward contract, for settlement in three-months' time, might be £1 = \$1.59. In this example, the forward value of the dollar against sterling is higher than its spot value by \$0.0100 or 1 cent (\$1.60 - \$1.59).

It might be supposed, if the current exchange rate is £1 = \$1.60 and the forward rate for settlement in three months £1 = \$1.59, that over the course of the next three months the spot rate should change from \$1.60 to about \$1.59. In practice, however, the forward rate is by no means always a reliable guide to future movements in the spot exchange rate.

Purchasing Power Parity Theory of Exchange Rates

Purchasing power parity (PPP) theory attempts to predict how an exchange rate should change over time. It is based on the argument that it should cost about the same to buy goods in one country as in another. For example, if a basket of goods could be bought for £1,000 in the UK and the same goods could be bought in the US for $1,500, the sterling/dollar exchange rate should be £1 = $1.50.

Purchase prices in each currency change with the rate of inflation in the domestic economy, and PPP theory predicts that exchange rates will vary over time because of differing rates of inflation in each country. In the example above, if the price of the basket of goods rose by 20% in the UK to £1,200 and by 12% in the US to $1,680, the exchange rate would change to £1 = $1.40 (1,680 ÷ 1,200). The dollar will strengthen against sterling because the rate of inflation is lower in the US than in the UK.

Measuring PPP Rates

PPP rates are measured. They are based on detailed price estimates carried out in each member country once every five years by the OECD. These price estimates can be used to establish PPP rates between currencies. The PPP rates can be adjusted in each intervening year until the next five-yearly prices measurement on the basis of the annual rate of inflation in each country. For example, suppose a PPP rate between the dollar and the Swiss franc is measured as $1 = SFr1.60. If inflation in the next 12 months is 2% in Switzerland and 4% in the US, the PPP rate will change to

$$\text{SFr}1.60 \times \frac{1.02}{1.04} \text{ to \$1, i.e. to } 1.5692$$

Reliability of PPP Rates

Some market analysts consider PPP rates to be a fairly reliable predictor of exchange rate movements over the long term. However, long-term movements are often difficult to predict because of large short-term fluctuations in market exchange rates. In some cases, market exchange rates have been out of line with the PPP rate for long periods of time.

PPP theory is attractive because it is a simple predictor of exchange rate movements. Unfortunately, although the PPP rate could be a broad guide to what the exchange rate ought to be, and a reasonable predictor of the exchange rate over the longer term, it is an unreliable predictor of exchange rates in the short-to-medium term. The volatility of market rates in the short term cannot be explained by differences in inflation rates; and in the medium-term, a variety of economic factors such as the government's interest rate policy, can keep a currency above or below its PPP rate against other currencies for quite a long time.

Monetary Models to Predict Exchange Rate Movements

A monetary model for predicting exchange rate movements is based on the view that exchange rates are determined by the growth in the domestic money supply in each country.

- If a country's domestic money supply is rising faster than the rate of real growth in the economy, price levels will rise and the currency will depreciate in value against other currencies.
- If a country's domestic money supply is fixed and the economy is growing, the country's currency will appreciate in value against other currencies.

A problem with monetary models is that they cannot be used to predict with accuracy

- how exchange rates will vary in the short term as domestic prices respond to a rise in the domestic money supply
- how much currencies will appreciate or depreciate in value.

However, models can be used to judge the probable direction, up or down, or exchange rates in the future, and assess currency risks accordingly.

Currency Exposures

Currency risk arises from the volatility of exchange rates, uncertainty about future exchange rate movements and the need to exchange foreign currencies in international trade and finance. Attempts to reduce exchange rate volatility through exchange rate systems such as the ERM, have had only temporary success: there is always the risk that the system will break down when it comes under financial pressures. Even monetary union in Europe, and the creation of a new international currency for all member countries of the union, does not eliminate currency risk between the currency of the union and currencies of countries outside it. Predictions of future exchange rate movements are inexact and not necessarily correct.

Currency risk therefore is an inevitable feature of international trade and finance. However, individual companies can take measures to avoid or reduce their own exposures to risk, i.e. hedge their exposures, provided they know what exposures they face and how large they could be.

In the following sections, the different types of currency risk will be considered.

Exchange rate risks can be categorized as

- transaction exposures
- pre-transaction exposures
- translation exposures
- economic exposures.

Transaction exposures relate to current transactions that will result in a currency cash flow. They are connected mainly with buying and selling between countries, although transaction exposures also can arise from financing transactions (interest and capital payments) and intra-group dividends from a foreign subsidiary to another group company. Transaction exposures affect cash flows as well as profits and can have fairly immediate consequences for both.

Pre-transaction exposures are contingent exposures that arise when a company commits to a price in a foreign currency for a sales or purchase contract that has not yet been agreed. If and when the contract is agreed, a transaction exposure will arise. Pre-transaction exposures arise, for example, from issuing price lists in a foreign currency, or tendering a bid for a contract quoting a foreign currency price.

Translation exposures are connected mainly with investing abroad and borrowing in foreign currencies. They affect a company's reported balance sheet and profit and loss account in its published accounts. Translation exposures also have implications for the consolidated accounts of a group.

Economic exposures relate to future, as yet uncontracted, transactions and are long-term in nature. Economic exposures can have strategic implications for a company but are more easily overlooked.

Classifying currency exposures into these categories helps to identify the most effective way of managing them.

Sources of Currency Exposures

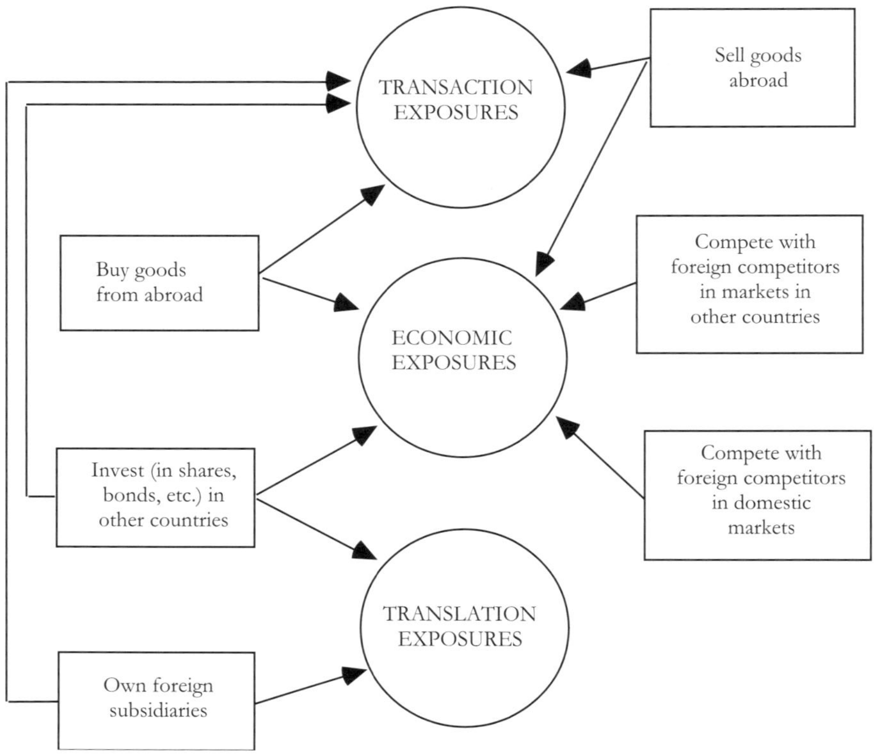

Transaction Exposures

Exposure to transaction risk arises when there is a specific arrangement to make a payment in a foreign currency or receive a payment in a foreign currency at some future time. The exposure lasts from the time the transaction is arranged, e.g. a sales contract is signed, until the payment is made or received. If exchange rates move adversely before the payment is made or received or the exposure is hedged, the company will have to

- pay more in its own currency to make a foreign currency payment, or
- receive less in its own currency from a foreign currency receipt.

Therefore cash inflows will be lower, or outflows higher, than expected.

Transaction Exposure for Currency Receivable

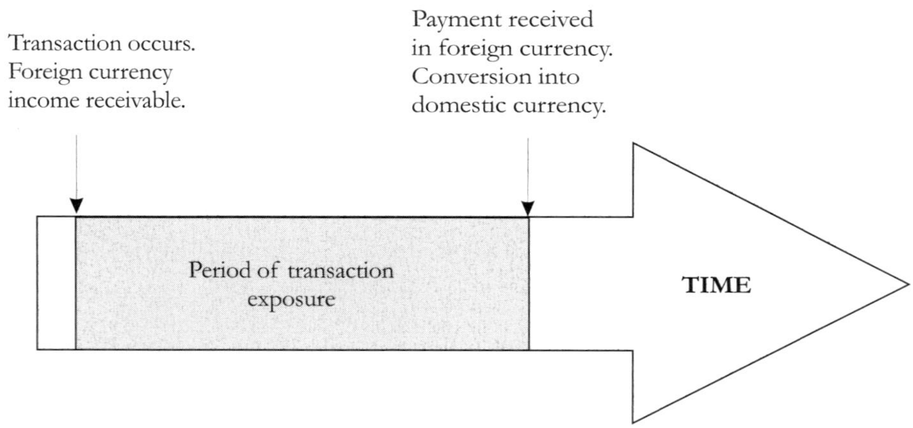

Transaction Exposure for Currency Payable

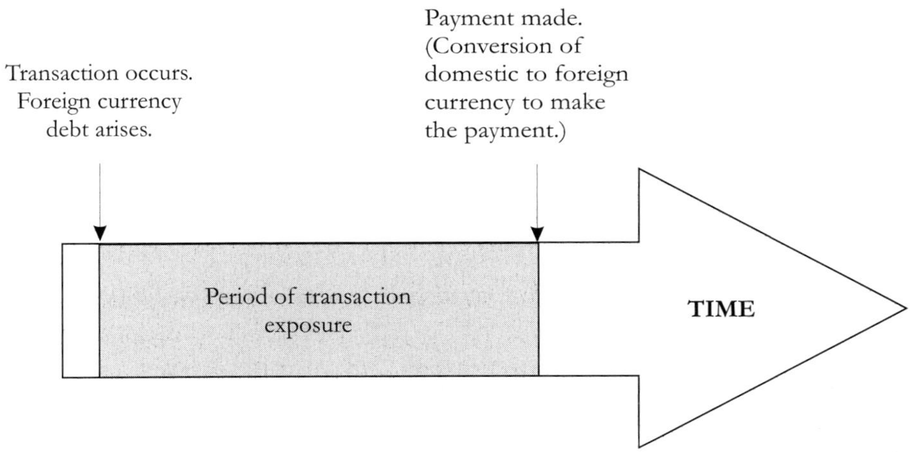

Example 1

A US company sells computer software on credit to customers in Spain and invoices in euros. A consignment for €90,000 of software has just been sent. The current exchange rate is €1 = $1.10.

Analysis

The company has a transaction exposure to a fall in the value of the euro. The exposure arises when the goods are sold on credit, and will end when the payment is received and converted into dollars. The company will sell the €90,000 it receives in exchange for dollars, and at the current rate of exchange would earn $99,000.

If the euro weakens before the payment is received, the actual earnings in dollars will be less than $99,000. Suppose, for example, that when the $99,000 is received, the exchange rate is $1 = $1.05. Earnings in euros will be $94,500, that is $4,500 less than expected.

Example 2

A UK company buys cheeses from France and pays in euros. It has no income in euros and buys the currency it needs from its bank to pay its suppliers. It has just bought a shipment of cheese for €15,000. The current exchange rate is €1 = £0.70. Payment is due in 60 days.

Analysis
The company has a transaction exposure to an increase in the value of the euro, arising from its debt to the cheese supplier. The exposure arises when the goods are ordered/delivered and ends when euros are obtained to settle the supplier's invoice.

When the shipment was bought, the company would expect the cost in sterling to be £10,500 at the current rate of exchange.

Suppose, however, that before payment is made, the euro strengthens in value against sterling to €1 = £0.75. The actual cost in sterling of the payment will be £11,250 that is £750 more than expected.

Example 3
A German company acting as agent for a Swiss supplier sells equipment to a customer in Dubai for $1.5 million. The company has agreed to pay the supplier SFr1.7million. If the current exchange rates are €1 = $1 and €1 = SFr1.70, the German company can expect to make a net profit of €500,000 on the transaction.

Sales income	($1.5m at €1 = $1)	1,500,000
Cost of sales	(SFr1.7m ÷ 1.7)	1,000,000
Profit		500,000

Analysis
The company is exposed to a fall in the value of the dollar during the period between making the sale and receiving payment because this would reduce its eventual income in euros. It also has an exposure to an increase in the value of the Swiss franc, between placing the purchase order with the supplier and paying for the equipment, because this would increase the amount it must pay in euros.

Transaction Exposures and Potential Losses

The previous examples show that when a company has an exposure to a foreign currency, the potential loss is not the full amount of the exposure. In the first example, the exporting company's transaction exposure to the euro was €90,000, from which it originally expected to earn $99,000. The potential loss was much less. If the euro fell in value against the dollar during the period of the transaction exposure by 1%, the loss to the exporter would be $990 (1% of $99,000). If the exchange rate were more volatile, however, and the euro fell by 10%, the loss would be $9,900. The euro would have to become worthless for the loss to be the full $99,000.

Similarly, in the second example, the importing company's transaction exposure to the euro was €15,000. Originally it expected the payment to cost £10,500 in sterling. The company's potential loss is much less than £10,500 because the euro/sterling exchange rate should be fairly stable, at least in the short term.

Loss from a Transaction Exposure

A transaction exposure puts a company at risk of a cash loss because an adverse movement in the exchange rate will mean paying more than expected or receiving less than expected, in domestic currency.

However, there is a problem in measuring the loss. The gain or loss from a currency exposure is the difference between the expected cash payment or receipt, and the actual cash payment or receipt.

- The cash that is eventually paid or received from the transaction is an actual, measurable amount of money.
- The expected payment or receipt, however, could be based on an exchange rate in the company's annual budget, or on the exchange rate prevailing at the time of the transaction, shipment date or invoice date.

Example

A UK company has bought a consignment of goods from a US supplier and has been invoiced for $60,000. The company purchases regularly from the US in dollars, and has assumed an average annual exchange rate of £1 = $1.60 in its budget.

The invoice was received a few days later, when the exchange rate was £1 = \$1.58. The company has no dollar income and buys the dollars it needs from its bank. When the payment was made to the supplier, the exchange rate was £1 = \$1.56.

Analysis
The actual payment was £38,461.54 (\$60,000 ÷ 1.56).

At the budgeted rate of exchange, the payment should have cost £37,500. At the rate of exchange on the invoice-received date, the expected payment was £37,974.68.

The loss on the transaction could be measured in either of the following ways.

	At budgeted exchange rate	**At invoice date exchange rate**
	£	£
Expected payment	37,500.00	37,974.68
Actual payment	38,461.54	38,461.54
Loss	961.54	486.86

The company's accounting department will record the exchange loss on the transaction as £486.86. This is because the invoice would have been recorded in the accounting system, in sterling at the exchange rate applying on the invoice date.

For management accounting and control purposes, however, it might be more appropriate to report a transaction loss of £961.54, depending on the requirements of the company's budgetary reporting system.

Exposures in Non-Convertible or Soft Currencies

If a currency is not freely convertible into other currencies, and is at risk to large devaluations, any significant income exposures in that currency would be a major financial risk. This is why many companies selling to customers in a country with a soft currency call for payment in a hard currency, such as the dollar.

Currency Exposures and Multinationals

Large multinational companies monitor their exposures in every major currency, including the domestic currency of their parent company. For example, the UK manufacturer British Aerospace must monitor its exposures in sterling because it manufactures primarily in the UK and has a UK-registered parent company. If it has large excesses of sterling expenditure over sterling income, the company would be exposed to an increase in the value of sterling because it would use income in other currencies, e.g. dollars, to pay for its sterling expenditures.

Transaction exposures sometimes can be disguised by shifting the exposures from the parent company to foreign subsidiaries through transfer pricing arrangements. This happens when a parent company exports through foreign distribution subsidiaries and the transfer price is fixed in the parent company's currency. Under such an arrangement the parent company sells its goods to foreign subsidiaries that sell them on to local markets.

Example
A UK parent sells goods in France through a French subsidiary and prices the transfer in sterling. The UK company might produce goods at a cost of £5 per unit in England and ship them to the French subsidiary at a price of £8, making a £3 profit. The subsidiary, having paid £8, might sell the goods for €15. The parent company, producing and selling goods in sterling, has no transaction exposures and its profit and loss account is untroubled by exchange gains or losses.

The foreign subsidiary, buying in sterling and selling in euros, acquires the exposures and the problem of exchange losses or gains. Although the parent company has shifted the exposures to its subsidiary, the exposures continue to exist within the group.

Pre-transaction Exposures

Pre-transaction currency exposures relate to transactions that have not yet taken place, but could occur at some time in the fairly near future. When and if the transaction occurs, the pre-transaction exposure becomes a transaction exposure.

A pre-transaction exposure arises when a company has already decided the foreign currency price at which it will buy goods from a supplier or sell to a customer, in fact before the purchase or sales transaction actually takes place.

- A company could decide to invest in an item of capital equipment, for which it will have to pay in foreign currency. Pre-transaction exposure lasts from the decision to buy until the order is placed, when it becomes a transaction exposure.
- A company could submit a tender for a major contract, pricing its bid in a foreign currency. A pre-transaction exposure will arise, lasting from the submission of the fixed price bid until the acceptance or rejection of the bid by the customer. If the bid is accepted, the exposure becomes a transaction exposure.
- A company exporting goods to a foreign market could issue a price list in foreign currency, where the prices are firm for a specified season/time period. By using a foreign currency price list, the company has continuing or recurring exposures for all its sales to the export market.

Continuing or recurring pre-transaction exposures have much in common with direct economic exposures.

Example

A Swiss company is asked to quote a price in dollars for supplying a consignment of goods on credit to a customer in the middle east. The company submits a price quotation of $100,000 on April 12, when the dollar/Swiss franc exchange rate was $1 = SFr1.54. Credit terms were 60 days net, i.e. payment was due in full 60 days from the invoice date.

The customer accepted the order on May 8. The goods were delivered and invoiced on May 25. The customer took over 90 days' credit, and paid on August 28.

During the year, the dollar had fallen in value against the Swiss franc, as follows

Date	$/SFr rate
May 8	1.5200
May 25	1.5100
August 28	1.4550

The Swiss company converts its dollar income into Swiss francs as soon as the income is received. The budgeted cost and the actual cost of the consignment were SFr120,000.

Analysis
A pre-transaction exposure arises on April 12 when the dollar-priced quotation is submitted. At the exchange rate on that date, the company would expect to earn Swiss franc income of SFr154,000 from the sale.

The pre-transaction exposure becomes a transaction exposure when the customer accepts the quotation and orders the goods (May 8), although the exposure does not affect the company's accounting records until the invoice is sent (May 25). Then the invoice will be recorded at SFr151,000 in the company's accounting system.

Following the fall in the value of the dollar, the eventual income from the sale is less than originally expected (SFr145,500), and the exporter has suffered a loss from the change in the exchange rate.

Transaction and Pre-transaction Exposure

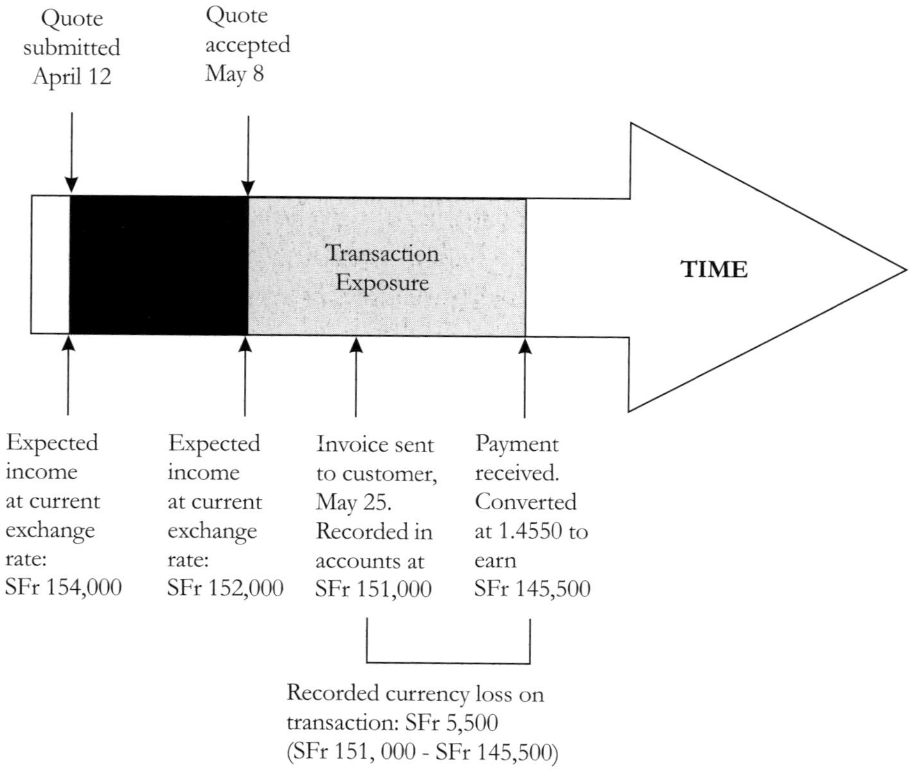

	Income	Cost	Profit
Expected profit, when price quotation submitted	154,000	120,000	34,000
Expected profit, when order received	152,000	120,000	32,000
Expected profit, when invoice sent	151,000	120,000	31,000
Actual profit	145,500	120,000	25,500

In this example, the company's profit from the sale is much less than originally expected because of the fall in the value of the dollar against the Swiss franc.

Conclusion

Transaction exposures are a risk to a company's cash flows. In some instances, the gain or loss from exchange-rate movements might exceed the profit or loss on the underlying trading transaction unless the company hedges the exposure.

Translation Exposures

Translation exposure is an oddity of financial accounting. It differs from transaction exposure because it does not relate to cash flows and the payments or receipts of money. It is a risk of losses, or lower profits, arising from preparation of the consolidated financial accounts of a company with foreign subsidiaries.

When a multinational prepares its consolidated accounts, the assets, liabilities and profits of foreign subsidiaries are translated from their local currency into the reporting currency of the group. For example, UK-based multinationals such as ICI or BP must translate everything into sterling in order to present their accounts. Such companies face a gain or loss on translation of the financial results of their non-UK subsidiaries because exchange rates alter between the start and the end of the financial year.

Translation exposures affect both

- the consolidated balance sheet of the group, and
- the consolidated profit and loss account of the group.

Translation Exposures and the Group Balance Sheet

A consolidated balance sheet for a group of companies shows the combined value of the assets and liabilities of all the companies in the group in the currency of the group's parent company. The assets and liabilities of each foreign subsidiary in the group therefore must be translated into the parent company's reporting currency.

The net investment in a foreign subsidiary is the balance sheet value of what the parent company owns, and is the difference between the subsidiary's total assets and its external liabilities. External liabilities are amounts owed by the subsidiary, excluding debts to the parent company and other companies in the group. The value of the net investment, translated into the parent company's domestic currency, will rise or fall with movements in the exchange rate.

Example
A UK company owns a US subsidiary and the net investment (assets minus liabilities) in the subsidiary at January 1 was $110.2 million. At the end of the year (December 31) the net investment in the subsidiary was unchanged at $110.2 million. The assets and liabilities of the subsidiary must be translated into sterling for the UK company's consolidated accounts, and the year-end exchange rate is used.

Analysis
If the dollar weakens, there will be a fall in the sterling value of the investment, and a loss on translation. The exchange rates at the beginning and the end of the year are as follows

January 1	£1 = $1.45
December 31	£1 = $1.52

The fall in the value of the net sterling investment would be measured as follows

Value of net investment		**£ million**
at January 1	($110.2m ÷ 1.45)	76.0
at December 31	($110.2m ÷ 1.52)	72.5
Loss on translation		3.5

The net investment remains at $110.2 million, but the sterling value of the net investment in the US company has fallen because of the exchange rate movement. The company has incurred a paper loss of

£3.5 million from its translation exposure to the dollar of $110.2 million. This is an accounting loss of £3.5 million, but not a cash loss.

Translation Exposures and Group Profits

The profits of a foreign subsidiary are consolidated into the group financial accounts by translating them at an appropriate rate or rates of exchange into the reporting currency of the parent company. Commonly the rate used is either the average rate for the year or the year-end rate.

The profits of a subsidiary, translated into the parent company's currency, could decline from one year to the next because of a fall in the value of the subsidiary's domestic currency, even though its reported profits in that currency are stable or have even increased year on year.

Example
A UK company has a US subsidiary that makes profits of $72 million every year. For the consolidated accounts, these profits are translated at the average exchange rate for the year. In Year 1 this was £1 = $1.50 and in Year 2 it was £1 = $1.60.

Analysis
The subsidiary's profits are $72 million each year, but translated into sterling, there would be a decline in profitability between Year 1 and Year 2 of £3 million.

		£ million
Year 1 profits	($72 million ÷ 1.50)	48.0
Year 2 profits	($72 million ÷ 1.60)	45.0

Decline in profits (as reported in sterling) 3.0

This decline in reported profits arises because of the dollar's fall in value against sterling.

Dividends and Retained Profits

If the foreign subsidiary makes no dividend payments out of profits, the parent company's exposure to the subsidiary's domestic currency has no implications for cash flow. However, a transaction exposure arises when a decision is taken to declare a dividend out of the subsidiary's profits. The dividend will be payable in the domestic currency of the subsidiary. On receiving the dividend, the parent company probably will convert the money into another currency. The transaction exposure arises from the intention to convert the dividend into another currency.

Example
A Japanese company's 100%-owned Dutch subsidiary made profits of €100 million. The profit is translated into yen for the purpose of preparing the group's consolidated accounts at the average rate for the year. This was €1 = ¥130. A final dividend of €40 million was declared. At the end of the group's financial year, the exchange rate was €1 = ¥125.

Analysis
The subsidiary's profit for the year, translated into yen, was ¥13,000 million.

Of the total profit, €40 million is payable to the parent company as a dividend and €60 million will be retained by the subsidiary. Because of the fall in value of the euro, the yen equivalent of these amounts at the year-end is as follows

		¥ million
Dividend	(€40 million x 125)	5,000
Retained profit	(€60 million x 125)	7,500
		12,500

The difference between the translated profit for the year (¥13,000 million) and the combined value at the year end of the proposed dividends and the retained profit (¥12,500) is a paper accounting loss, arising from the fall in value of the euro and the group's exposure to the euro.

The group's exposure to the euro remains. Profits of €100 million can be separated, however, into a transaction exposure and a continuing translation exposure. As at the year-end, the parent company has

- a transaction exposure of €40 million for the dividend receivable, and
- an additional translation exposure of €60 million for the profits retained by the subsidiary.

The transaction exposure will end when the dividend is paid and the euros are converted into yen by the parent company. The translation exposure will continue indefinitely, so long as the profits are retained by the subsidiary.

Profit Histories and Profit Forecasts

When a parent company has a currency exposure arising from its investment in a large foreign subsidiary, both its reported profits and its expected profits will depend on the exchange rate. If stock market investors believe that the domestic currencies of a parent company's subsidiaries will weaken in value, expectations for group profits will fall. The parent company's share price probably will fall as a consequence.

Currency Risks from Investing in a Foreign Subsidiary

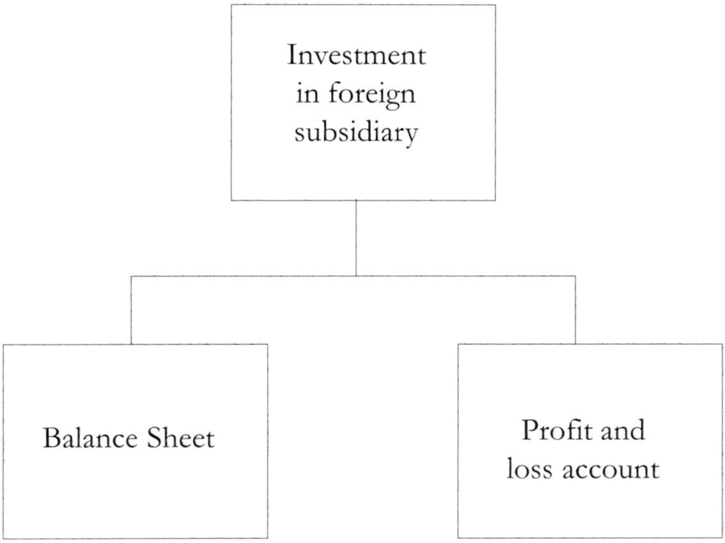

Translation exposure

Net investment in subsidiary varies with movements in the exchange rate

- Translation exposure for retained profits
- Pre-transaction exposure, where annual dividends are expected
- Transaction exposure, for dividends that are declared
- Dividends expected by parent company shareholders could be affected by foreign subsidiary profits. Therefore the parent company share price could be vulnerable to weakness in the currency of its foreign subsidiary

Example
A UK-based multinational group earns most of its annual profits from the activities of subsidiaries in the US and Hong Kong. The profits of these subsidiaries, in dollars and Hong Kong dollars, are expected to rise by a small amount next year.

The parent company's shares have a London stock market listing.

Analysis
Most of the group's profits are earned in dollars and Hong Kong dollars, and the UK-based group has a large exposure to these currencies. If these currencies were to fall in value against sterling next year, the reported profits of the group would fall.

The shareholders of the parent company will receive an annual dividend in sterling. The money to pay the dividend will come mainly from dividends paid in dollars to the parent company by its US and Hong Kong subsidiaries. A weakness in the dollar or the Hong Kong dollar therefore could affect the amount of dividend that the parent company could afford to pay.

In these circumstances, the share price of the UK parent probably would fall because of investor concerns about future dividends.

Conclusion

Parent companies have translation exposures whenever they own foreign companies. As a result, the balance sheet value of a group can be reduced by adverse exchange rate movements and increased by favorable movements.

These gains and losses on foreign currency may not have any effect on the group's cash flows and many translation exposures simply give rise to paper currency gains or losses in the consolidated accounts of the group. Interestingly, some multinationals take the view that because their shareholders are choosing to invest in a broadly based portfolio of worldwide businesses, company policy on the management and control of its currency risks should not be determined by such paper profits or losses. Therefore an active policy of hedging against translation exposures would be inappropriate.

The risk from translation exposures should be far less serious than transaction exposures, unless group profits rely heavily on the profits and cash dividends from foreign subsidiaries, particularly when the subsidiaries are based in countries with weak currencies.

Economic Exposures

When a company buys or sells abroad regularly, there is a continual risk of diminishing revenues, or mounting costs because of adverse exchange rate movements. These on-going or long-term currency risks are called economic exposures.

International trade creates economic exposures for

- any company that incurs costs in one currency and earns income in another, and
- any company that competes in its markets with foreign rivals, and not just companies exporting goods or services to foreign markets, but also companies facing foreign competition in their domestic markets.

Any change in exchange rates between currencies will improve or worsen a company's financial and market position.

Types of Economic Exposure

In the context of currency risk, economic exposure refers to the implications of exchange rate movements for any *future* contracts and transactions that might occur in a company's business. Economic exposures are long term and potentially are the most damaging manifestation of currency risk. They can have profound implications for the strategy of global companies.

There are two main consequences of economic exposures.

- Exchange rates have an impact on the revenues or costs of future production. If exchange rates move adversely, a company will suffer a reduction in profits because of lower income or higher costs (imported materials) from future transactions. These economic exposures are *direct*.
- If exchange rates move adversely, a company also will forfeit a degree of price competitiveness to foreign producers. These economic exposures are *indirect*.

Direct Economic Exposures

Direct economic exposures are currency exposures that will arise in the future from a company's trading transactions. For example, a UK-based jewelry maker has an on-going need for gold, a commodity denominated in dollars. A strengthening of the dollar will raise the price of gold in sterling, affecting the UK jeweler's prices, or profit margins, on future output. So long as the jeweler continues to produce in the UK, and incur expenditures in sterling, direct economic exposures will exist.

Direct economic exposures eventually will become transaction exposures when future production and sales become current and the amount of an exposure is known exactly as a contracted amount to be received or paid.

Example
A US trader imports optical equipment from Switzerland, priced in Swiss francs. The equipment is resold to US customers, who pay in dollars.

Analysis
The trader has direct economic exposure to the Swiss franc. If the dollar declines against the Swiss franc, he will have to pay more in dollars to obtain his equipment supplies. If the decline is long term, he will have to pass on his higher costs to customers by raising prices, or accept a permanent reduction in profit margins. If he raises his prices, sales volume could fall as customers switch, perhaps to equipment supplied from Mexico or Poland.

This long-term exposure is a result of direct economic exposure to adverse exchange rate movements. Economic exposure of this sort becomes a transaction exposure for the US company whenever the specific contract to import is made. A company facing direct economic exposures, by pricing its goods in a foreign currency or by purchasing supplies in foreign currency, will face a continual stream of transaction exposures in the normal course of its trading.

Direct Economic Exposure and Pre-transaction Exposures

Direct economic exposures are similar in many respects to pre-transaction exposures. Direct economic exposure relates to future transactions for which prices may not have been fixed, whereas pre-transaction exposures relate to future transactions for which the price has been fixed by price list or contract tender.

For example, a company begins foreign operations and commits itself to a series of payments in a foreign currency for set-up costs.

- When the strategic decision is taken to expand, the company takes on a direct economic exposure to the currency.
- When a decision is taken to make a particular investment in equipment, a pre-transaction exposure arises.
- When the equipment is purchased on credit the pre-transaction exposure becomes a transaction exposure that lasts until the equipment is paid for.

Indirect Economic Exposures

Indirect economic exposures, sometimes called strategic exposures, refer to the implications for cost- and price-competitiveness of exchange rate changes. A significant change in the sterling/euro rate, for example, will affect the relative competitiveness of German and UK producers. A fall in value of most currencies against the euro, for example, will have a substantial adverse effect on the global competitiveness of many companies in the euro zone. Similarly, a UK company exporting electronic goods priced in sterling might compete in international markets with Japanese suppliers who price their goods in yen. If the yen weakened against sterling, the UK exporter would become less price competitive while Japanese exporters would become more price competitive.

The earlier example of the US trader importing Swiss optical equipment illustrated direct economic exposure to the Swiss franc for the trader. The Swiss supplier, faced with lower-price competition from Mexico or Poland, has indirect economic exposures to the Mexican peso and the Polish zloty. A rise in the value of the Swiss franc could result in a switch of demand in US markets to rival goods made in Mexico or Poland.

Even if a company doesn't trade or invest abroad, there is still an economic currency risk. For example

- a downturn in the domestic economy will affect a local company more than a similar company with subsidiaries abroad where there might be a stronger economy
- competitor firms might trade abroad, achieving higher sales and profits, and improving cost efficiency with higher output volume. This would enable them to improve their competitive edge at the expense of rival companies without an export presence
- foreign companies with lower costs can compete by supplying rival goods. During the late 1990s many US industries suffered because of competition from cheap imports that resulted from a strong dollar.

Changes in exchange rates affect the relative costs of producers in different countries. If a UK producer, for example, paying its costs in sterling competes in world markets with a German producer, whose expenses are in euros, their comparative costs of production will be affected by changes in the euros/sterling exchange rate. Any such changes will affect the ability of either the UK or the German producer to compete effectively, depending on which way the exchange rate moves.

Example 1

The effect of economic exposures on competitiveness can be illustrated by a simple example. Suppose that world markets are dominated by two producers, one US, one French. The products of both firms, however, are priced in dollars.

	US company	**French company**
Revenue	100% in dollars	100% in dollars
Costs	100% in dollars	100% in euros

- The economic exposures of the French company might seem fairly clear. If the euro increases in value against the dollar, the euro value of its dollar earnings will fall and its profit margins will be squeezed.
- In a competitive sense, however, both companies are exposed to currency risk. A stronger euro will make the French company less profitable, and the US competitor will be in a better position to hold prices down and win larger market share. For the same reason, an increase in the value of the dollar against the euro will give the French company a competitive edge.

This exposure to cost competition would disappear if both companies were to produce in the same country or in countries in the same currency bloc. In this example, the French company might be tempted to shift production facilities to the US if it suspects that the euro will be overvalued against the dollar in the long term.

Example 2

A UK car producer competes mainly with German car producers in both its home and export markets and management is concerned about the company's economic exposure to the euro/sterling exchange rate. So it decided to purchase gearboxes, one of its most expensive components, from a German supplier. By making this decision, the UK company incorporates euro expenditures into its cost structure, reducing its economic exposure to the euro/sterling rate.

Economic Exposures and Price Sensitivity

The price sensitivity of a product is an additional factor in the context of economic exposures. A price-insensitive product will not be affected by economic exposures. For example, a pharmaceuticals company might manufacture a unique and successful drug in its laboratories in Sweden. If the product were in such strong demand that customers worldwide would buy it at almost any price, the company's economic exposure to changes in the value of the Swedish krona would be negligible. If the krona increased in value, the drug would cost more to foreign buyers, but they would pay the higher price, and the company's sales and profits would remain intact.

A totally price-insensitive product does not exist, however, and even products with no direct competitor, such as the Boeing 747 airplane, have a price above which market demand will fall.

By contrast, for those products whose demand is highly sensitive to price changes, economic exposures to exchange-rate variations can be vitally important in international markets. For example, suppose that the demand for drill bits is price-sensitive, and that the world market is dominated by rival producers in Spain and Mexico. The Spanish producer would be exposed to an increase in the value of the euro and to a fall in the value of the Mexican peso against other world currencies. Because any such change would make the Mexican-produced goods relatively cheaper, customer demand would shift from Spain to the Mexican manufacturer.

Products competing in particularly price-sensitive markets, such as most commercial airplanes, semi-conductors or calculators, require extremely careful management of inherent economic exposures merely to compete.

Such exposure management should seek to ensure that the manufacturer is at least in a position of competitive parity with overseas suppliers in terms of currency exposures. It can then compete on efficiency and unit cost of production.

Problems arising from indirect economic exposures call for strategic solutions such as the relocation of plants, sourcing supplies from different countries, diversifying the customer base into other countries or financing operations in different currencies.

Gains and Losses from Exposures

Many companies face all types of currency exposure: transaction, translation and economic. The diagram opposite illustrates the position of a UK car manufacturer, exporting cars produced in the UK through a US distribution subsidiary for sale in dollars to the US market.

- Transaction exposures arise because production costs are mainly in sterling but income is in dollars.
- Translation exposures arise from the net investment in the US distribution company.
- Economic exposures are both direct and indirect. Direct exposures relate to future sales in the US market. Indirect exposures relate to the relative price/cost competitiveness of the UK producer against rival producers in the US, Japan, Germany, or France.

Potential Cost of Currency Exposures

Currency exposures create a two-way risk. Favorable movements in exchange rates will result in profits from the exposures, just as adverse rate movements cause losses.

Potential Exposures Facing a Company

Stage 1: UK production costs in sterling

Stage 2: shipment to US

Stage 3: sale to US distribution subsidiary in dollars

Stage 4: sale to retail customer in dollars

TRANSACTION EXPOSURE arising from the sale of cars in dollars but production costs in sterling

TRANSLATION EXPOSURE on profits and asset of US distribution company

ECONOMIC EXPOSURE on future uncontracted car sales to the US, and costs of German competition sourced in euros, or Japanese competition

Exchange Rate Risk: Possible Consequences

Transaction exposure

Risk of lower cash income or higher cash spending

Risk of lower profits and earnings and lower earnings per share

Translation exposure

Group balance sheet risks:
Reduction in the reported value of overseas assets or increase in the cost of foreign currency liabilities, leading to a lower net worth

Group profit and loss account risks
Risk of lower reported profits and lower earnings per share

Economic exposure

Risk or erosion of competitive advantage

Risk of lower market share

Risk to long-term profitability

Because a currency exposure can result in a profit if the exchange rate moves in a favorable direction, and a loss only if the movement is adverse, it could be argued that currency transaction exposures should not be a cause for concern. Over time, if the exchange rate fluctuates up and down around a central value, gains and losses on exchange rate movements should be roughly in balance.

In practise, however, the harmful impact on a European company of an exchange loss of €20,000 from a transaction exposure could be greater than the beneficial effect of an exchange gain of €20,000. The company could have cash flow problems if its cash income falls, or if it has to pay more to settle foreign currency debts.

As a result of this many companies take the view that

- if there is a reasonable probability that an exchange rate will move favorably, exposures in the currency can be tolerated, but
- if it is uncertain how an exchange rate could vary, measures should be taken if possible to hedge the exposures, especially if the exchange rate is volatile.

Small Companies

For many small companies exporting goods or services or buying from abroad, foreign currency transactions often involve small-value deals. But for the company the transaction exposure from small deals could be significant, particularly when the number of small-value transactions is quite large. There is still a risk of lower-than-expected profits because of adverse exchange rate movements. Even small companies could benefit from a system of identifying their foreign currency transaction exposures, and taking hedging measures to reduce the risk.

Some banks offer computerized dealing systems to customers that allow them to trade in foreign exchange for low-value transactions without having to phone the bank to make the transaction. Ready access to a foreign exchange dealing system can help companies hedge transaction exposures efficiently.

The examples that follow illustrate the types of exposure that can arise in different situations, and the potential or actual loss in each case.

Example 1: Selling Abroad in Foreign Currency
A UK company has sold capital equipment to a customer abroad for \$116,000. At the time of shipment, the sterling/dollar exchange rate was £1 = \$1.45. Payment is received three months later, when the exchange rate is £1 = \$1.60.

Analysis
The company had a transaction exposure to a fall in the value of the dollar. The dollar fell in value during the period of exposure, resulting in a lower inflow of cash and lower profits than originally anticipated.

		£
Sterling value of sale at time of dispatch	(\$116,000 ÷ 1.45)	80,000
Sterling eventually received	(\$116,000 ÷ 1.60)	72,500
Shortfall in cash and profits from the sale		7,500

Example 2: Selling Abroad in Domestic Currency
A US company sells goods to several countries, particularly Germany. It can produce the goods for $8 each and sell them for $11 or their equivalent in foreign currency.

Analysis
The company has indirect economic exposure to a rise in the value of the dollar against other currencies. If the dollar strengthens over time, there could be a fall in demand in foreign markets, and a consequent fall in profits as the company's products become less competitive against those of foreign producers. A fall in the value of the dollar will improve the company's competitiveness.

For example, suppose the euro/dollar exchange rate is €1 = $1.05 in January Year 1, but in August the dollar falls in value, so that €1 = $1.15. As a result the US company immediately would become more competitive in German markets. If its dollar prices to German buyers remain unchanged, the cost to buyers in their own currency, the euro, would have fallen by about 10% just because of the change in the exchange rate. Sales demand from German customers probably would rise significantly.

Suppose that from August Year 1, the dollar recovers some of its value, and in early January Year 3, stands at around €1 = $1.10. This rise in the dollar's value will erode some of the US producer's cost advantage over German rivals. If the dollar strengthens even further in value against the euro, from €1 = $1.15 to €1 = $1.10, a German customer will have to pay €10 for the company's product instead of €9.57 for a US product priced at $11. Demand for the US company's output in Germany is likely to fall unless the company responds by lowering its prices to $10.50 perhaps and accepting a smaller profit margin per unit.

Example 3: Buying from Abroad in Foreign Currency
A Dutch company has purchased photocopiers from Japan at an agreed price of ¥15,600,000. At the time of delivery, the exchange rate was €1 = ¥130, but by the time payment was due the exchange rate had changed to €1 = ¥120.

Analysis
There is a transaction exposure between the time of purchase and delivery of the photocopiers when the company is at risk to a rise in the value of the yen. In this example, the risk materialized and the company had to pay more in sterling than it originally anticipated.

		¥
Cost in euros of purchase at time of sale	(15.6m ÷ 130)	120,000
Euros eventually paid	(15.6m ÷ 120)	130,000
Cash payment above original expectation		10,000

Annual profits of the company also will be lower over the life of the photocopiers because depreciation charges, based on a purchase cost of €130,000 rather than €120,000, will be higher.

Example 4: Investing Abroad
A UK-based company has a large French subsidiary. At January 1, the exchange rate between the euro and sterling was €1 = £0.70.

The group's balance sheet was

	£
UK business assets	9,100,000
French subsidiary assets (€13,000,000)	9,100,000
	18,200,000
Financed by:	
Equity capital	9,100,000
Loans (in sterling)	9,100,000
	18,200,000

In the year to December 31, the UK operation made no profits and just broke even.

The French subsidiary made profits of €1,000,000, but paid no money in dividends to the UK parent company. The exchange rate at December 31 was €1 = £0.65.

At some point the French subsidiary is likely to pay dividends to the UK parent company. What further exposure does this create for the company?

Analysis

There is translation exposure. The French subsidiary has earned profits in euros, and within the eurozone of countries these are unaffected by exchange rate movements. However, the UK parent company must report the profits and balance sheet value of its French subsidiary in sterling within its own published consolidated accounts in the UK. The consequences of translation exposure emerge from the conversion of euro values into sterling.

The consequences of the exposure and the rise of sterling against the franc are as follows

A reported loss on translation

		£
Value of French subsidiary at January 1	(€13,000,000x0.70)	9,100,000
Re-translated at 31 December exchange rate	(€13,000,000x0.65)	8,450,000
Loss in value on translation		650,000

Lower profits

Profits reported in sterling are lower than if the exchange rate had not changed. If the exchange rate had stayed at €1 = £0.70, the value of the €1,000,000 profits in sterling would have been £700,000. Instead, the reported profits are only £650,000.

Lower equity in group balance sheet

Consequently, a lower equity value is shown in the group's consolidated balance sheet than if the exchange rate hadn't changed, and the group will have a higher financial gearing ratio. Financial gearing, defined simply, is the ratio of debt capital to equity shareholders' capital, and high gearing in a company's capital structure is an indication of potential financial weakness.

The year-end balance sheet is

	£
UK business assets	9,100,000
French subsidiary assets (€13,000,000 + 1,000,000) x 0.65	9,100,000
	18,200,000

Equity capital	£
At January 1	9,100,000
French subsidiary profits (1,000,000 x 0.65)	650,000
Loss on translation (see above)	- 650,000
At December 31	9,100,000
Loans in sterling	9,100,000
	18,200,000

In this example the profits earned by the French subsidiary have been wiped out by the loss on the foreign exchange movement.

If the exchange rate had stayed at €1= £0.70, the group's assets at December 31 would have been £700,0000 higher, at £18,900,000, and the value of equity would have been £9,800,000.

The French subsidiary probably will pay dividends, in euros, to its UK parent each year. There is an economic risk that if the euro were to fall in value against sterling in the long term, the sterling cash value of dividend payments, as well as the sterling value of the subsidiary, would fall. Between the time that a dividend is declared and the time that it is paid, a transaction exposure to the euro will arise for the UK parent.

Example 5: Borrowing in a Foreign Currency
A Hong Kong company wants to borrow HK$12,000,000. The rate of interest on a Hong Kong dollar loan would be 7% per annum, so the company decides instead to borrow €1,500,000 and convert this into Hong Kong dollars. The exchange rate is €1 = HK$8, and interest on a euro loan is only 4%. The loan is for two years.

Analysis
The company has both transaction exposures and translation exposures. The risk is that the euro might increase in value against the Hong Kong dollar.

Transaction exposure arises from interest rate payments and the repayment of the borrowed capital. At €1 = HK$8, the company would need HK$480,000 each year to meet the annual interest payments of €60,000, and the cost of paying off the loan at the end of the second year would be HK$12,000,000. If the euro strengthened against the Hong Kong dollar, the Hong Kong dollar cost of payments would rise. At an exchange rate of €1 = HK$9, for example, the company would need HK$540,000 to meet the annual interest payment and HK$13,500,000 to repay the loan.

Translation exposure arises from the need to report the cost of outstanding loans in Hong Kong dollars in the company's published accounts. If the full loan of €1,500,000 were still outstanding at the company's year-end, and the exchange rate were €1 = HK$9, the loan would be reported as a creditor for about HK$13,500,000, with a reported loss on translation of HK$1,500,000 because the original HK$ value of the creditor at €1 = HK$8 was only HK$12,000,000. Eventually, the loan must be repaid, and so this translation exposure also can be described as long-term direct economic exposure that will become transaction exposure when the loan matures.

The end result is that as the euro rises in value, the total cost of the euro loan to the Hong Kong company could possibly exceed 7%, the interest rate at which the company could have borrowed in Hong Kong dollars.

An Approach to Managing Currency Risk

Management is generally risk adverse, and often will take measures that reduce or eliminate exposures that could have a harmful effect on its business. A risk-avoidance measure is known as hedging the risk or the exposure.

It is important to recognize that currency exposures could create potential losses, and every company ought to establish

- whether it has any currency exposures and in what currencies?
- If so, what kind of risks are involved and how do they arise?
- Are they significant and should they be hedged?

Even if exposures are not hedged, management should ensure that they are regularly monitored to ensure that the risk does not increase to the point where potential losses could be significant.

Managing Financial Risk: Monitoring Exposures

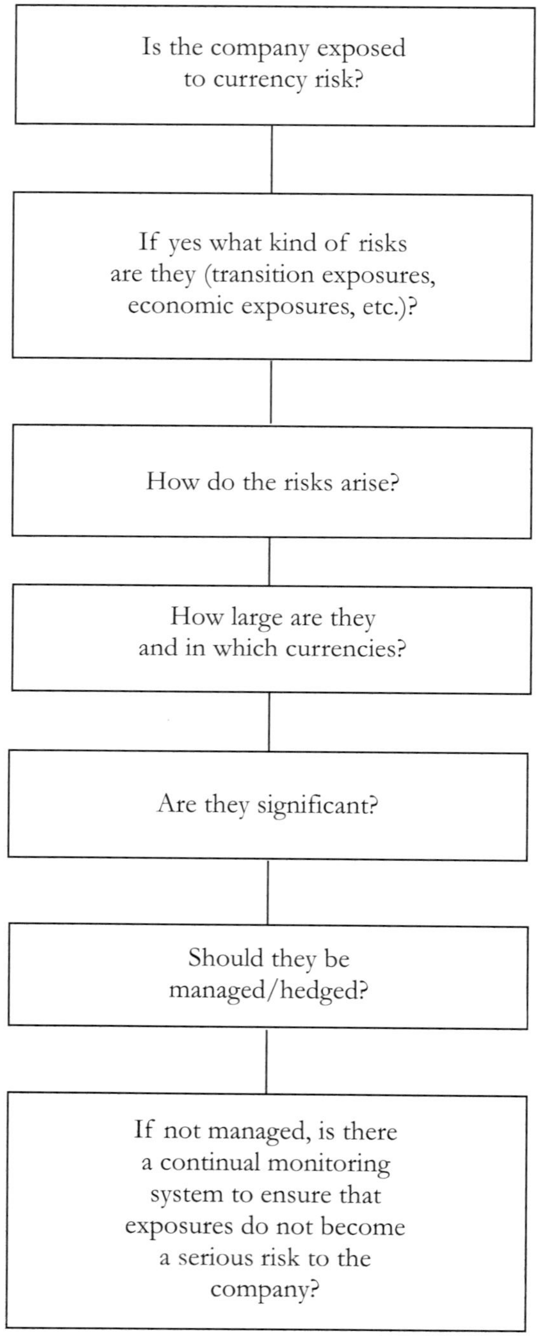

Identifying and Quantifying Exposures

In devising a strategy for managing exchange rate risks, a company must

- *identify* what exposures it has, or may acquire, and
- *quantify* the exposures to assess their significance.

Identifying Exposures

Identifying exposures is both a strategic and an operational requirement. A strategic review can identify economic exposures, but a day-to-day system for recognizing transaction exposures as they arise also should be in place.

Transaction exposures are fairly easy to identify because they are specific amounts of money receivable or payable in foreign currency. Similarly, translation exposures exist whenever a company owns a foreign subsidiary, and also are readily apparent.

Identifying Economic Exposures

Competitive exposures are long-term and difficult to quantify. However, companies with economic exposures need to recognize the risks their businesses could face from foreign competition. They also could attempt to assess how a change in the exchange rate could weaken their competitive position.

Indirect economic exposures can be more difficult to identify for two main reasons.

- Often they are long-term exposures whereas the planning horizon of many organizations is mainly short term.
- They depend on the future actions of foreign competitors and the potential effect of exchange-rate changes on their relative cost-competitiveness. For example, it is easy to overlook the risk that a long-term increase in the value of the euro against the Canadian dollar might attract more competition from Canadian suppliers into the domestic markets of the euro-zone countries, as well as making output from Canada relatively cheaper than rival European products in other markets around the world.

In any market, indirect economic exposures always will exist whenever there is a foreign competitor.

The following examples illustrate the broad approach to identifying and analyzing economic exposures.

Example 1
A UK-based multinational company owns a hotel chain in the US. The hotel chain earns most of its revenues and incurs most of its expenditures in dollars. Its main competitors are also US-based.

Analysis
The UK company has no significant economic exposure to the dollar from its ownership of the US hotel chain because its income and its expenditures are both mainly in dollars. However, there could be translation exposures because of its ownership of a dollar-valued subsidiary, and some transaction exposures, for example arising from dividend payments from the US subsidiary to the UK parent.

Example 2
In 1987 there was a sharp fall in the value of the dollar. French wine producers chose to maintain their prices in francs for exports to the US. As a consequence, US consumers switched to cheaper Californian wines. The growth in the Californian wine industry in turn led to more wine exports from the US to Europe.

Analysis
French wine producers failed to recognize their economic exposure to a weak dollar, and took no price-cutting action to protect their US markets. Their failure to take a strategic price-cutting measure resulted in greater competition from Californian producers in the US and Europe.

Quantifying Transaction Exposures

As soon as a company contracts to make a foreign currency payment or to acquire a foreign currency receipt at a future date, a transaction exposure is created. Existing transaction exposures are easily quantified: they are the amount of the receipt or payment.

A company with regular foreign currency receipts or payments should establish a routine procedure for estimating future transaction exposures over six months or a year.

Estimates of transaction exposures should be made for each main currency in which the company has receipts or payments, and should be updated regularly.

Four important elements in estimating transaction exposures are

- the currency of the exposure
- the amount of the exposure
- the time period of exposure
- the direction of the cash flow: receipt or payment?

These elements can be shown graphically. A contract worth $120,000 to a UK company is illustrated opposite with an exchange rate of £1 = $1.50 at the contract date.

The time frame of the exposure is the period between the formalization of the contract and the date when receipt or payment occurs. During this time, the potential gain or loss from movement in the sterling/dollar exchange rate is shown for variations between £1 = $1.40 to £1 = $1.60.

Exposure to Currency Loss or Gain

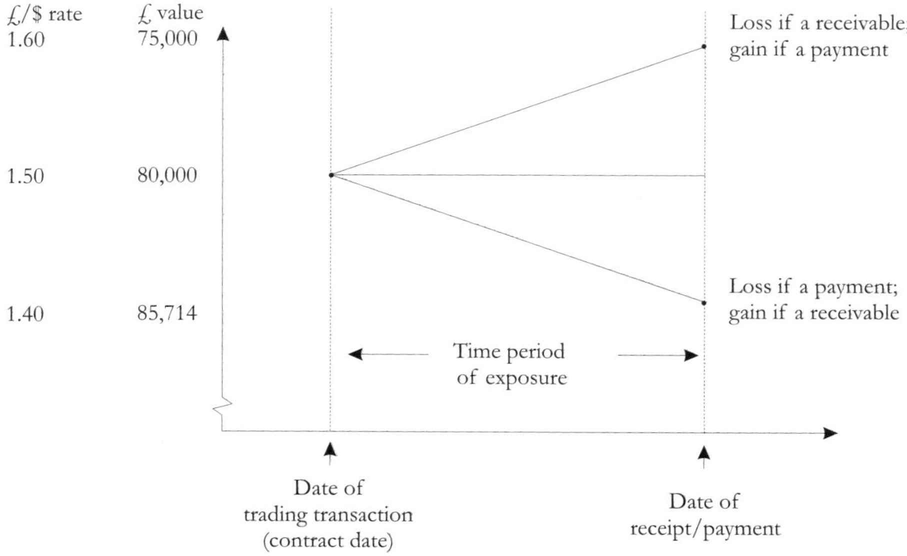

Dividing Exposures into Time Slots

Unless a company has taken hedging measures, the size of its transaction exposures in any currency is the total of its future known receipts in that currency (revenue exposures), and its future known payments in that currency (payment exposures). Exposures can be divided into time slots according to when the currency receipts or payments will occur.

Example
A German company expects to receive income in dollars from several customers during the next 12 months. The anticipated timing and amounts of receipts are

	$
February	600,000
April	1,000,000
June	400,000
October	2,000,000
November	500,000
	4,500,000

Analysis
These exposures could be expressed as an annual dollar income of $4,500,000. Alternatively, depending on the company's budget and control systems, the exposures could be divided into

- monthly time slots, with dollar income in each month as shown
- quarterly time slots, with dollar income exposures of $600,000 in the first quarter to the end of March, $1,400,000 in the second quarter to the end of June, nothing in the quarter to the end of September, and $2,500,000 in the final quarter
- half-yearly time slots, with $2,000,000 income in the first half of the year and $2,500,000 in the second.

Preparing a Cash Flow Forecast

To quantify total exposures in any currency, a cash flow forecast should be prepared, showing committed and estimated receipts and payments.

- A forecast is needed for each currency in which the company has cash flows.
- The forecast should cover several months, up to one year perhaps, but a new rolling forecast should be prepared regularly, i.e. monthly or weekly, depending on the frequency of transaction exposures.
- The forecast can show future cash flows by day, by week, or by month. Daily or weekly estimates might be used for committed cash receipts or payments in the short term, and monthly or quarterly estimates for projected and therefore uncertain long-term transactions.

Example: Estimate of Currency Receipts and Payments January-June
Currency: dollars in 000s

	January	**February**	**March**	**April-June**
Trading receipts	1,400	1,800	2,400	9,600
Intercompany receipts (dividend capital receipts)		400		
Total receipts	1,400	2,200	2,400	9,600
Trading payments	(1,700)	(4,200)	(1,800)	(7,000)
Intercompany capital/ interest payments	(200)			(300)
Total payments	(1,900)	(4,200)	(1,800)	(7,300)
Net exposure (positive or negative)	-500	-2,000	600	2,300

Assessing Transaction Exposures

The size of a net exposure will allow a company to gauge the financial risk it faces. In the example a $2,000,000 excess of expenditure over receipts in February would put the company at risk to a rising dollar between now and then. An increase in the value of the dollar from €1 = $1.10 to €1 = $1.00 during the time period of exposure would alter the euro value of a net payment of $2,000,000 from about €1,818,182 to about €2,000,000, an increase in expenditure of €181,818 for the month.

Quantifying Economic Exposures

The forecasting of economic exposures, both in the short and long term, presents a more exacting task.

Short-term Economic Exposures
Estimates of future transaction exposures, referred to earlier, are actually estimates of short-term direct economic exposures. A distinction can be

made between *certain* direct economic exposures and *potential* exposures by currency for each time period in the forecast.

There also might be pre-transaction exposures arising from tendering for contracts abroad and from price lists in foreign currencies.

- If a company tenders for contracts in foreign currency, it should estimate its cash flow exposures during the period between the tender and the awarding of the contract, as well as between the contract and receipt of payment.
- If a company issues overseas price lists in foreign currency, it should estimate future exposures for the duration of the price list's validity.

The precise quantification of economic exposures inevitably will involve a degree of informed supposition. An on-going exposure can be divided into core, or certain exposure and non-core, or optional exposure.

Example

A UK-based civil airplane manufacturer knows that because the dollar is the pricing currency for civil airplanes, its production always will create dollar revenues, and a continuous economic exposure will arise. The only issues are

- How many airplanes will be produced?
- At what dollar price will they be sold?

The company could estimate that over the next three years it will produce between 15 and 20 airplanes that will sell for between $20 million and $25 million each.

Analysis

The core exposure to the dollar is 15 x $20 million = $300 million. This is the minimum output at the minimum price; $300 million represents the company's minimum dollar income over the period, on the basis of the assumptions used. The company could decide to hedge this exposure.

The non-core exposure is $200 million (20 x $25 million minus the core exposure of $300 million). This exposure may not arise. If the company wishes to hedge the non-core exposure, it would most probably choose a conditional hedge, using currency options or other such products.

Long-term Economic Exposures

Long-term economic exposures are even more difficult to quantify precisely. However, some attempt should be made at measurement because large exposures could indicate an urgent need to revise business strategy.

Measuring long-term economic exposures should begin with an assessment of future markets for the company's products, the competition, and the currencies in which the products will be sold and the costs incurred.

Market Size: Annual Sales

Forecasts of future markets should attempt to predict the total market, and assign a proportion of it to each country (currency). The total market might be either the entire world market, or the company's own predicted sales turnover. The table below indicates estimates that might be made for a UK-based company.

	Total sales ($ equivalent)	**Sterling**	**Dollars**	**Euros**	**Swiss francs**
	million	million	million	million	million
World market	1,500	150	800	600	100
Company's own sales	450	90	300	30	0

In this example, the company expects to have a 30% share of the total world market, with much of its sales in dollars – the largest part of the world market – and a predominant position in sterling-based markets.

In contrast, it expects to have only a 5% share of the market for sales in euros, and no sales in Swiss francs. This would indicate that the company has a significant economic exposure to changes in the sterling/dollar rate, quantifiable as $300 million of sales income per annum. This analysis is incomplete however, because to quantify economic exposures totally would require an analysis of the currencies of expenditure for both the UK company and its competitors.

Cost Structures

Cost structures can be projected for the company, and possibly also for its competitors, in the currency of its costs. If raw materials are imported, the currency of costs will not be 100% domestic currency. Similarly, a company with overseas production facilities will incur costs in a variety of currencies.

A table of costs, using this same example, might be as follows

	UK company	**Competitor A**	**Competitor B**	**Competitor C**
	%	%*	%*	%*
Sterling	70	0	0	0
Dollar	30	35	100	40
Singapore dollar	0	65	0	0
Euro	0	0	0	60
	100	100	100	100

* *estimate*

Some analysis of economic exposures can be obtained by comparing these cost structures. The UK company in this example is the only producer with expenditures in sterling (70% of its total spending). Therefore it is exposed to an increase in the value of sterling against the dollar, the Singapore dollar and the euro.

- If sterling strengthened against the Singapore dollar, the company would lose some cost-competitiveness against Competitor A that has 65% of its expenditure in Singapore dollars.
- Similarly, if sterling strengthened against the euro, the company

would lose some of its cost-competitiveness against Competitor C.

- If sterling were to strengthen against the dollar, the UK company would suffer a loss of cost-competitiveness against all three that have a greater proportion of their spending in that currency, but in particular against Competitor B.

In the same way Competitors A, B and C all have exposures to a fall in the value of sterling that would improve the UK company's competitiveness against them. Exposures create the potential for gain as well as the risk of loss.

Net Economic Exposure Analysis

A net economic exposure is the difference between income and expenditure in a currency over a defined period of time. Because exchange rate movements create an equal and opposite currency gain or loss for an equal amount of income and expenditure, financial risk arises only from the net amount of exposure in each currency.

By considering the probable future size of the markets in each currency in conjunction with cost structures, it should be possible to estimate the size of a company's net economic exposures, year by year, in each currency.

Using the same example, the company's net exposures that are the difference between expected annual revenue and expenditure are as follows

	Revenue	**Expenditure**	**Exposure**
Sterling	£90 million	£155 million	- £65 million
Dollar	$300 million	$130 million	+ $170 million
Euro	$30 million	–	+ $30 million

These are expected to become transaction exposures at some time in the next year.

Here the company has economic exposures to an increase in the value of sterling against the dollar and the euro. A fall in the dollar's value from £1 = $1.50 to £1 = $1.60 could cost the company about £7 million for the year ($170 million ÷ 1.50) - ($170 million ÷ 1.60).

Similarly, a fall in the value of the euro from €1 = £0.70 to €1 = £0.65 would cost the company about £1,500,000 each year (€30 million x 0.70) - (€30 million x 0.65).

Identifying the True Currency of Exposure

Identifying the currency of exposure inherent in a particular transaction or business is not always straightforward. Sometimes the currency of denomination and the currency of exposure are different.

For example, a German company regularly requiring a dollar-based commodity such as oil or gold does not eliminate its exposures by asking its supplier to invoice in euros. Although transaction exposures can be avoided by making the supplier convert prices into euros, thus shifting responsibility for currency risk management up the value chain to the supplier, economic exposure to the dollar remains. The net effect is to

- mask the true currency of exposure. The company still has an exposure to the dollar despite paying for its supplies in euros. All the supplier will do is apply the prevailing market rate for the euro/dollar to its dollar prices in order to quote prices in euros to the German customer.
- increase the supplier's prices to reflect the currency transaction executed on the customer's behalf. If the euro weakens, the supplier will increase his euro-denominated prices.

Similarly if a UK airplane producer were negotiating to sell airplanes priced in sterling to a British airline company, the producer would still have an indirect economic exposure to the dollar because the dollar is the main pricing currency in the civil aircraft market. The British airline company would compare the sterling prices quoted by the UK producer against the dollar prices of rival international manufacturers.

Quantifying Translation Exposures

Translation exposures are unrelated to cash flow. The total exposure is the parent company's net investment in its foreign subsidiaries. The size of potential losses depends on exchange rate volatility over time.

Effect on the Profit and Loss Account

The annual profits of a foreign subsidiary are included in the group's total profits for the year by translating them into domestic currency values at either an average exchange rate for the year, or the year-end (closing) exchange rate.

Profits earned overseas, when translated, are worth

- more if the foreign currency strengthens against the reporting currency during the year, or
- less if the foreign currency weakens in value.

For example, if the profits of a Hong Kong subsidiary of a UK company are HK$24 million, the reported profits in the group's financial accounts will be £2.4 million if the exchange rate is £1 = HK$10, but only $2 million if the rate is £1 = HK$12 .

Effect on the Balance Sheet

A group's balance sheet will include the various assets and liabilities of foreign subsidiaries, usually translated at the year-end rate of exchange.

Increases or falls in the value of the foreign subsidiary are reported in the group's financial accounts as gains or losses on foreign currency translation. When they occur, there is a twofold effect. There is an increase or decrease in the value of the group's net assets, and there is a matching increase or decrease in the group's equity reserves in the balance sheet.

Example

A US subsidiary of a UK company had assets of $7,830,000 million at December 31 Year 1, and a loan of $3,480,000. During the year to December 31 Year 2, it made a profit of $840,000 and paid no dividend.

Exchange rates	**£1=**
December 31 Year 1	$1.45
Year 2 average	$1.60
December 31 Year 2	$1.75

Analysis

The company's translation exposures are the annual profits and the net asset value of its foreign subsidiary, i.e. $840,000 and $7,830,000.

The UK company can choose to translate the profits of its foreign subsidiaries into sterling at either the year-end exchange rate or at an average rate for the year.

The group's profits for the year, as reported in sterling, will vary according to the exchange rate used. In this example, there is a £45,000 difference, and because the value of the dollar declined over the year, the group's profit will be higher if the average rate of exchange is used.

	Using average rate (÷ 1.60)	Using year-end rate (÷ 1.75)
Subsidiary's Year 2 profit of $840,000, in sterling	£525,000	£480,000

Although the company's profits for the year will differ according to the exchange rate used, the end result in the balance sheet is the same. There will be an increase or, as in this example, a decrease in the group's net assets and reserves caused by the change in the exchange rate during the year. The amount of this increase or decrease will differ according to the exchange rate used to report profits by the amount of the profit difference.

It will be useful to note how these losses or gains make their way into the group's balance sheet.

The subsidiary's net assets at the *start* of the year were $4,350,000.

	$
Assets at start of year	7,830,000
Minus loan	3,480,000
Net assets at start of year	4,350,000

The sterling value of these assets changes with fluctuations in the exchange rate, and there is a fall in value, an exchange loss, between the start and end of the year.

		£
Net assets translated at start-of-year rate	(÷ 1.45)	3,000,000
Net assets translated at year-end rate	(÷ 1.75)	2,485,714
Loss on translation		514,286

If the subsidiary's profits are translated at the average yearly exchange rate, there is a further gain or loss on translation. This occurs because the sterling value of the dollar profits will have changed by the end of the year to their year-end rate value.

		£
Sterling value of profits at average rate	($840,000 ÷ 1.60)	525,000
Sterling value of profits at year-end rate	($840,000 ÷ 1.75)	480,000
Further loss on translation		45,000

Here again there is a variation in reported profits because of exchange rate movements. The subsidiary's profits were earned in dollars, and it is only their sterling equivalent value that is changing.

The net effect on the balance sheet can be summarized as follows

	Exchange rate used to translate profits	
	Average rate	Year-end rate
	£	£
Profits for the year (add to reserves)	525,000	480,000
Losses on translation		
Translating start-of-year net assets	(514,286)	(514,286)
Translating profits for the year	(45,000)	
Net change in balance sheet	-34,286	-34,286

The change in the balance sheet can be presented in another way.

	$		£
Net assets at start of year	4,350,000	(÷1.45)	3,000,000
Add profits (after any dividend)	840,000		
Net assets at end of year	5,190,000	(÷ 1.75)	2,965,714
Change in net assets			-34,286

Assessing the Significance of Exposures

The significance of a company's exposures depends on

- the size of the exposure
- the probability of favorable or adverse rate movements and,
- the likely size of any adverse rate movement.

Assessing the risk leads to the key issue of whether a company's management should take measures to limit and control it.

Risk Management Strategies

Most businesses are exposed to currency risk. Even the small producer for a local market often will be threatened by cheap foreign imports, a form of indirect economic exposure.

Potential Costs and Benefits of Exposures

The potential costs and benefits of exposures can be assessed quite easily, provided the exposures have been quantified. This assessment calls for a simple judgment about the possible change in the relevant exchange rate. Transaction exposures and translation exposures should be analyzed separately.

Example 1

A company based in Spain has estimated that during the next year, it will earn income of \$10.5 million and will have expenditure of £2.1 million. The current exchange rates are €1 = \$1.05 and €1 = £0.70, so that expected income from dollar sales is €10 million, and expected spending on sterling purchases is €3 million.

It is anticipated that the average euro/dollar rate over the next year could rise or fall by up to 15%. Similarly, the view is taken that the average euro/sterling rate over the next year might fluctuate by up to 5%.

Analysis

As a result of the volatility in the euro/dollar exchange rate, potential euro income from dollar sales could be about €1.5 million higher or lower than estimated (15% of €10 million), and this would have a direct impact on company profits. Similarly, the company's expenditure might be up to €150,000 higher or lower than estimated because of the possible volatility in the euro/sterling rate.

Example 2
A US company owns a Dutch subsidiary that has a net asset value of €20 million and earns annual profits of €3 million. The current exchange rate is €1 = $1.08.

Analysis
Translated into dollars at the current rate of exchange, the value of the company's net assets is $21.6 million, and annual profits are $3.24 million (3 million x 1.08). A 5% movement in the exchange rate, up or down, would result in the dollar value of the net assets changing by $1,080,000, and reported annual profits changing by $162,000.

Choosing a Currency Risk Management Strategy

Currency risk is a two-way risk because exchange rate movements can be either favorable with a resulting gain, or adverse with a resulting loss. A company might take the view that currency risk is acceptable whenever it occurs, and that gains or losses on exchange rate movements should be tolerated because over the long term they should cancel each other out. This attitude to currency exposures is considered risk neutral.

Risk neutrality might be a suitable strategy to adopt when the potential cost or gains are small relative to the size of the company's business and profits. For example, suppose a UK company earns annual income of about £30 million and $0.9 million, and expects annual profits to be about £6 million. There is some currency exposure with the dollar income. If the current exchange rate is £1 = $1.50, the dollar income would yield £600,000 at the current rate, and a fall in the value of the dollar by 20% would cost the company £120,000 in lost annual income. In relation to total profits of £6 million, the currency risk might seem tolerable. On the other hand, if the same company expected annual profits on the same turnover of only £500,000, the currency exposures might cause greater concern.

If the potential losses and gains from exchange rate movements are high in proportion to expected trading profits, a company should be less inclined to take a risk-neutral attitude, and ought to consider ways of managing the risk.

Risk management involves

- avoiding risk whenever possible where significant losses might occur
- controlling risk if it cannot be avoided altogether to minimize the size of potential losses
- tolerating the risk, or even adding to exposures when exchange rate movements are more likely to be favorable than adverse.

A suitable strategy towards currency exposures is suggested on page 96.

Taking measures to avoid or minimize the risk from exposures is called hedging. The terms hedging the risk and hedging the exposure mean the same.

Management of currency risk implies that the company is not risk neutral. A company is *risk averse* if measures are taken to minimize the exposures, and *risk seeking* if measures are taken to increase exposures to profit from favorable exchange rate movements.

The aim of hedging is to reduce or eliminate the risk from adverse exchange rate movements. A consequence of hedging is either

- having to incur additional expenditure to hedge the exposure, or
- forgoing the opportunity to make a profit if there is a favorable movement in exchange rates.

Hedging therefore has a cost, or a potential cost. Companies accept the costs of hedging as the price to pay for reducing the risk of losses.

Controlling Currency Risk

There are several ways in which a company might seek to control its currency risks.

- Transaction exposures can be avoided by refusing to buy or sell except in domestic currency.
- Translation exposures can be avoided by refusing to establish foreign subsidiaries.
- The threat that foreign competition might benefit from exchange rate movements (indirect economic exposure) and be able to be countered by measures to improve productivity, reduce output costs and become more cost competitive.

Hedging Choices

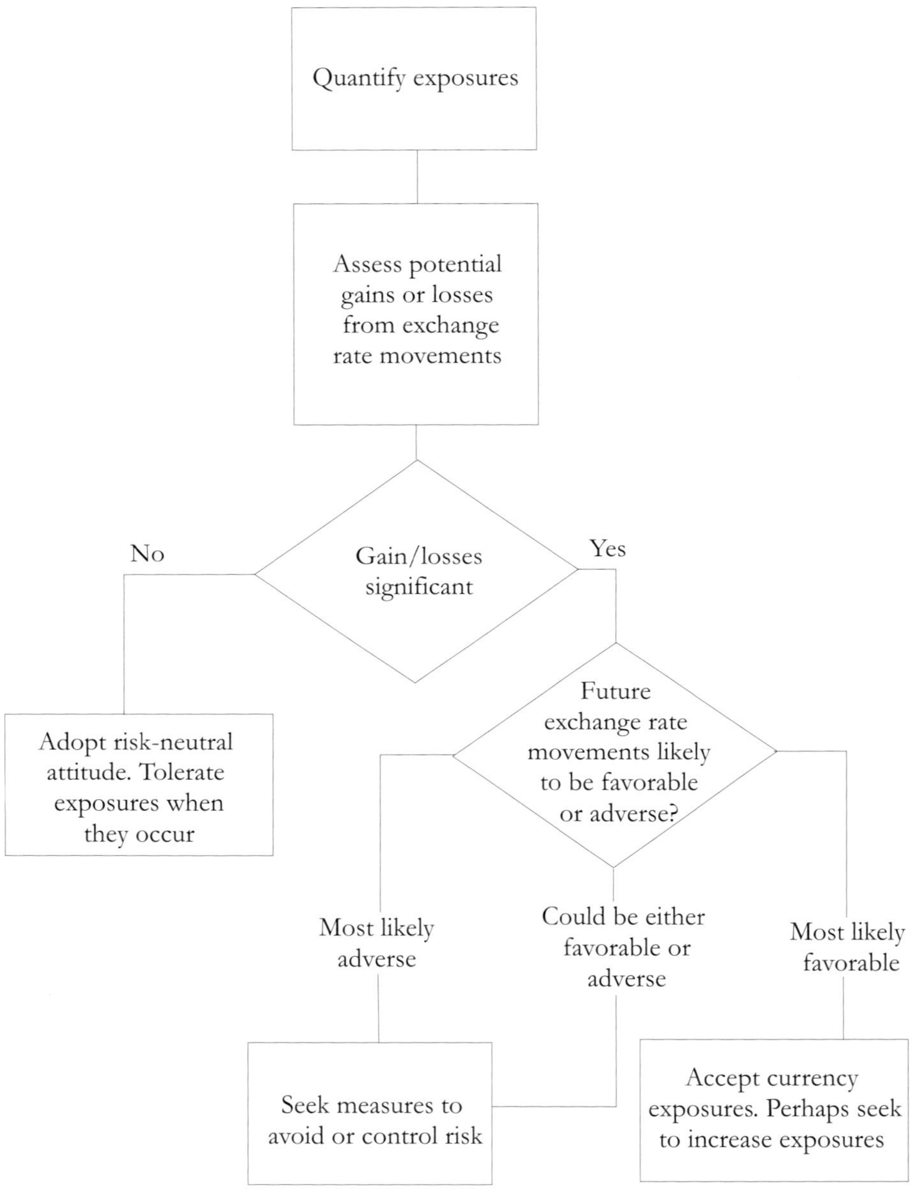

Many small businesses can protect themselves from currency exposures by adopting these measures. A French company with no foreign subsidiaries that prices its output and settles its accounts in euros, and is continually trying to improve efficiency and productivity, ought to have only limited exposures, even from foreign competition.

For many companies, currency exposures cannot be controlled in such a simple way. They must buy goods from abroad and pay in foreign currency, or must accept payment in foreign currency for export sales. Large companies must seek to develop their business in world markets by setting up subsidiaries abroad. As international trade develops and markets become more global, companies will face increasing currency exposures, and other measures should be adopted to control them.

Measures to hedge currency exposures have evolved over recent decades, and companies including banks, can choose which hedging methods to use. These include measures such as forward contracts, options, futures and swaps. Some basic issues underlying hedging techniques are introduced below.

Hedging Transaction Exposures

Avoiding risks from transaction exposures will involve measures that eliminate the uncertainty about the actual rate of exchange between the time the transaction is made and the time when the currency is bought or sold. These measures include

- refusing to buy or sell in foreign currency, an approach that was discussed earlier. It avoids having to convert one currency into another
- having an income and expenditure in the same currency. This avoids the risk by using the income to pay for the expenditure without converting the foreign income into domestic currency. For example, a Spanish company that earns \$500,000 and spends \$500,000 can use the income to make the payment, without having to convert dollars into euros or euros into dollars. Matching income and expenditures in the same

currencies is called *structural hedging*. It can be done only by companies with income and expenditure streams in the same currency. Furthermore, it is often difficult to match incomes and expenditure exactly

- preventing variations in the future exchange rate by fixing now the rate for future transactions. Several financial instruments have been developed to make this possible. The most widely used are forward exchange contracts. Borrowing in foreign currency, currency swaps and currency futures are other financial instruments that achieve, in differing ways, much the same result
- preventing adverse variations in the future exchange rate without avoiding exposures to *favorable* variations that would result in gains. This is achievable with currency options.

In practise, many companies

- hedge all their net exposures from trading transactions, for which firm sales or purchase orders have been made, and in addition
- take hedging measures for a proportion, perhaps 50-75%, of export sales that are expected to happen over the next 6-12 months or so but have not yet become firm orders.

Hedging Translation Exposures

Translation exposures arise whenever a company has a foreign subsidiary. The exposure arises from the net assets the parent company owns that are denominated in a foreign currency. These exposures can be reduced, if required, by minimizing the amount of net assets in the foreign currency. Because net assets are the difference between total assets and total external liabilities, a reduction in net assets can be achieved by borrowing money in the foreign currency, thus increasing total liabilities.

Foreign currency borrowing is a common method used by multinational companies to restrict translation exposures.

Increasing liabilities in a foreign currency, e.g. by borrowing, without any increase in assets would imply a smaller equity investment in that particular country, as shown in the following diagram where the exposure is represented by the shaded box.

Hedging Exposures by Borrowing

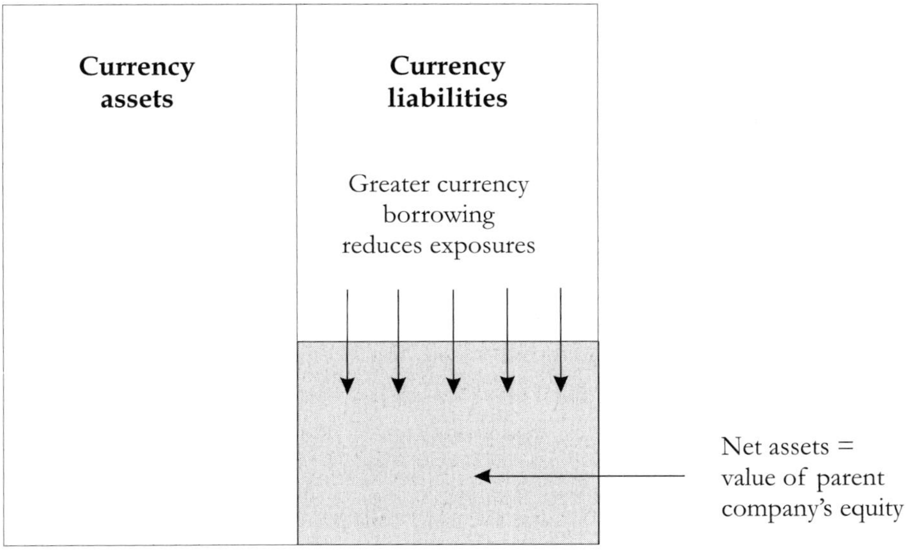

Accepting or Increasing Currency Risk

Where a company considers that the future movement in a particular exchange rate is almost certain to be favorable, it might decide to accept whatever exposures that may arise in that currency without taking measures to hedge them. At the same time, it might hedge exposures in other currencies where there is a greater likelihood of adverse rate movements.

For example, if a US company believes that the Japanese economy is fundamentally stronger than the US economy and the yen is likely to strengthen over time, it could decide not to hedge a constant stream of yen receivables in order to benefit from this anticipated revaluation.

Speculating

Currency speculation is the opposite of hedging. It involves deliberate measures to increase currency exposures in the expectation that future exchange rate movements will be favorable.

For example, a UK company that expects the dollar to decline against sterling might decide to borrow heavily in dollars. The company might borrow $27 million when the exchange rate is £1 = $1.50 and then convert the dollars into £18 million. If it anticipates that when the loan is repaid, the exchange rate will be £1 = $1.80, it will need only £15 million to repay the loan principal.

In the currency markets, opportunities for speculation are varied, but a non-financial trading company normally should avoid such speculation because its objective should be to earn profits from selling goods or services, rather than from gambling on foreign currency movements. Occasionally, however, some companies speculate in currency for profit. It is difficult to know how often this happens because companies aren't required to disclose their risk management strategies.

However, there have been occasional reported cases of the treasury department of a large company increasing the company's transaction exposures in a particular currency and suffering heavy losses when the exchange rate failed to move in the anticipated direction. In reported cases, the currency speculation by individuals in the treasury department appears to have been unauthorized.

For example, some years ago Showa Shell Sekiyu, a Japanese affiliate of the Royal Dutch/Shell group, reported unrealized foreign exchange losses of about $1 billion following speculation by its treasury department on the dollar/yen exchange rate. The treasury department gambled incorrectly on the dollar appreciating in value against the yen.

Currency Speculation by Investors

Some investors speculate on currency movements, buying or selling currencies in the hope of making a profit from favorable exchange rate movements.

Example
An investor has £1 million in sterling, and decides to speculate on currency movements through spot market transactions in foreign exchange markets.

Analysis
Suppose the investor believes the Swiss franc is about to increase in value against sterling. The investor could sell sterling in exchange for Swiss francs at a rate of £1 = SFr2.40. He will now have SFr2.4 million.

Next, he might decide to buy dollars, in the belief that the dollar is about to appreciate. He might sell all his Swiss francs at $1 = SFr1.50, buying $1,600,000 million (2.4 million ÷ 1.50).

By this time, the sterling/dollar exchange rate might be £1 = $1.55. If the investor wishes to convert his dollars into sterling, these would earn £1,032,258 ($1.6 million ÷ 1.55), yielding a profit on this speculative trading of about £32,000.

Speculating on currency movements sometimes can be based on well-informed predictions, when a particular currency is expected to collapse because of economic conditions and financial pressures. However, speculation also can be a form of gambling, similar in many respects to gambling money in a casino.

Banks and Currency Exposures

Measures companies can take to control currency risk often will involve arrangements with financial institutions and in particular banks. Forward exchange contracts, currency loans, options, futures and swaps are all obtainable from banks, or with a bank acting as broker or intermediary in the arrangement.

Although it is probably easier to understand currency risk and exposures for a non-bank company, it is important to recognize that banks also face the same problems.

Banks have their own currency exposures that arise from

- foreign currency loans and deposits, accepting foreign currency deposits from customers, lending foreign currency to customers
- buying and selling currency in the foreign exchange markets
- trading with customers in other financial instruments, such as options, swaps and futures.

Like other companies with potentially large exposures, banks will seek to control their risks, and to this end will use hedging techniques on their own accounts. Indeed, most of the trading in the currency markets is between banks.

Conclusion

The purpose of this book has been to describe the nature of currency risk and to suggest how the risks can be quantified and assessed. Risk management, as it is most normally applied, involves a risk-averse approach. It also involves adopting measures to control the risk, such as using forward exchange contracts and derivative products such as currency options, futures and swaps.

Glossary

Bretton Woods Agreement
A currency agreement reached at Bretton Woods, New Hampshire in 1944 that set fixed exchange rates for major currencies based on the convertibility of dollars into gold at a fixed price, and provided for central bank intervention in the foreign exchange markets to maintain the fixed rates. The system eventually collapsed in 1971.

Commercial Risk
The risk of profits being affected by unexpected changes in trading conditions.

Convertible Currency
A currency that can be freely exchanged for other currencies without permission from the central bank of the currency's country. Trading in convertible currencies is the function of the foreign exchange markets. Convertibility is limited when the foreign exchange market for that currency is illiquid.

Counterparty
One of the participants in a risk management contract, e.g. currency swap.

Country Risk
Legal, regulatory, political, economic and other risks involved in cross-border transactions with the country concerned.

Currency Clause

A clause in an export contract in which the sum payable is denominated in the buyer's currency; but the amount payable will vary with the exchange rate for the buyer's currency against the seller's currency. In this way, the exporter is not exposed *directly* to exchange risk that is borne by the buyer, even though invoiced in his own currency.

Currency Markets

The markets for transactions, largely inter-bank transactions, involving the exchange, purchase and sale or borrowing and lending of currencies.

Economic and Monetary Union (EMU)

The union established by several countries of the European Union (Austria, Belgium, the Netherlands, Luxembourg, France, Germany, Spain, Italy, Ireland, Finland and Portugal), that introduced the euro, a common currency, in January 1999.

Economic Exposure

Exposure to the risk that changes in exchange rates over the long term could favor the products of a competitor.

Economic Hedge

A measure taken to offset the advantage of a competitor with a depreciating currency. Could involve strategic measures such as relocation of production facilities or supply sources.

Eurocurrency

Currency deposited with a bank outside the currency's country of origin. Dollars held with a bank in London, Frankfurt or Hong Kong, for example, are eurodollars. Eurocurrency deposits are used for re-lending by banks in the international borrowing/lending markets known as the eurocurrency markets.

European Monetary System (EMS)

A set of rules agreed by member countries of the European Community, now the European Union, establishing the European Currency Unit (ECU) and Exchange Rate Mechanism (ERM). The EMS was the forerunner of EMU.

Exchange Controls
Government regulations restricting or forbidding certain types of foreign currency transaction including purchases from abroad, payment abroad of interest or dividends, and investing abroad by the country's nationals.

Exchange Rate Mechanism (ERM)
A part of the European Monetary System that sought to limit the volatility of exchange rates of member currencies.

Exposure
A financial risk facing a business that can be categorized according to its cause or source. Currency exposures are exposures to exchange rate risk.

Financial Risk
The risk of profits being affected by unexpected changes in financial conditions or circumstances.

Fixed Rate
An exchange rate between two currencies that is fixed at a specific level.

Floating Rate
An exchange rate between currencies that moves up or down according to demand and supply in the foreign exchange markets. A *clean float* responds to normal pressures of supply and demand, with little or no central bank intervention. A *managed float* occurs when a government, through its central bank, intervenes in the FX market either to stabilize its currency, or to allow it to move in a required direction (appreciate or depreciate).

Foreign Exchange Markets (FX Markets)
The markets for buying and selling foreign currency.

Forward Premium
The difference between the spot rate for a currency and its forward rate.

Forward Rate
Exchange rate at which a currency can be traded in the foreign exchange market, i.e. bought or sold for delivery/settlement at a specified date in the future, e.g. one month forward, three months forward.

Hard Currency
A currency whose value is expected to remain stable or increase in terms of other currencies.

Hedging
Taking action to reduce or eliminate an exposure, usually at the expense of potential reward. Currency hedging techniques include offset hedging, forward contracts to buy or sell currency and the use of derivative products such as options and swaps.

Leads and Lags
Process of accelerating (leads) or slowing up (lags) foreign exchange payments or receipts when a change in exchange rates is expected.

Market Risk
Exposure to adverse price changes in a market.

Netting
The practise of offsetting payments against receipts and using other hedging techniques only, such as forward cover for the net difference between payments and receipts. Also called offset hedging.

Price Risk (Market Risk)
The risk of a fall in the market value of a foreign investment, as measured in the domestic currency of the investor, due to an adverse change in the value of the currency of the investment.

Purchasing Power Parity (PPP) Theory

The proposition that over the long term, changes in the exchange rate between two currencies are the result of differences in the relative rate of inflation in the countries concerned. For example, if the current exchange rate between the Japanese yen and sterling is ¥ = £1, the exchange rate in one year's time should be

$$¥ \quad x \quad \frac{(1 + j)}{(1 + s)}$$

where j and s are the rates of inflation, expressed as a proportion, in Japan and the UK respectively.

Regulatory Risk

Risk that a law or regulation will conflict with an intended transaction, and prevent the transaction occurring.

Risk Neutrality

An attitude that risks should be neither sought nor avoided, but should be accepted whenever they arise.

Settlement

Process by which a transaction is recorded, and obligations between the parties are settled, e.g. by cash payment.

Soft Currency

A currency that is expected to devalue or depreciate against other currencies, or whose exchange rate must be supported by central bank intervention or exchange controls.

Speculation (Currency Speculation)

Buying or selling currency in the expectation of an exchange rate movement, so as to make a profit, either in the same market or between two different markets, e.g. FX cash markets and derivatives markets.

Spot Market
A market for immediate delivery and cash settlement, as distinct from a market for future delivery and settlement.

Spot Rate
The exchange rate at which one currency can be traded in exchange for another currency in the foreign exchange markets, for delivery/settlement in two working days.

Strategic Exposure
See Economic Exposure

Structural Hedging
The process of reducing or eliminating foreign currency exposure by matching receivables and payables in each currency or currency bloc to minimize the net exposure.

Transaction Risk
Currency risk for the period between a transaction occurring and the time when payment in foreign currency is made or received.

Translation Risk
Currency risk affecting the value of balance sheet assets and liabilities, and the reported profits of foreign subsidiaries.

Volatility
A measure of the tendency of a market price or yield, e.g. an exchange rate, to vary over time. Volatility is high when the price changes by a large amount over a short period of time. Volatility can be measured statistically as the annualized standard deviation of price changes.

Index

Notes

Notes

Notes

Notes

Notes

Notes